SISTAHS IN COLLEGE

SISTAHS
IN
COLLEGE

MAKING A WAY OUT OF NO WAY

Juanita Johnson-Bailey

KRIEGER PUBLISHING COMPANY
MALABAR, FLORIDA
2001

Original Edition 2001

Printed and Published by
KRIEGER PUBLISHING COMPANY
KRIEGER DRIVE
MALABAR, FLORIDA 32950

Copyright © 2001 by Krieger Publishing Company

Library of Congress Cataloging-in-Publication Data

Johnson-Bailey, Juanita.
    Sistahs in college : Making a way out of no way / Juanita Johnson-Bailey.— Original ed.
      p. cm.
    Includes bibliographical references.
    ISBN 1-57524-074-2 (hard)
      1. African American women—Education (Higher) 2. African American women—
Social conditions. 3. African American women—Interviews. I. Title.

    LC2781 .J59 2000
    378.1'9822—dc21

                                 00-020684

10 9 8 7 6 5 4 3 2

Dedication

This book is in tribute to a long unbroken line of Black women,
in whose arms I have found comfort,
in whose eyes I have found encouragement,
and in whose hearts I have found a place.

CONTENTS

FOREWORD

The lives of African American women are complicated by a variety of factors that combine to make them *conspicuously invisible* in many contexts. Their absence in representative numbers from the ranks of students, tenured faculty and administrators in the academy is taken for granted; commonly regarded as a fact of university life that has no foreseeable remedy. *African American women are not seen because they* ***are not*** *there.* Ironically, in those few academic situations where African American women have a significant presence, they routinely are ignored and unnoticed. *They are not seen because they* ***are*** *conspicuously invisible.* Regardless of whether or not this paradox is an accident, statistical data is not a sufficient means of understanding the dilemma of African American women in the academy, especially those older, "nontraditional" women who return to college as adults. Women's own words provide a more accurate barometer of life-shaping events both within and outside of the boundaries of higher education. Juanita Johnson-Bailey's *Sistahs in College: Making a Way Out of No Way* does just that—it opens the readers' eyes to the stark reality of African American women reentering the university community.

Previous studies of African American women in the academy tended to emphasize historical aspects of their education and few were based on women's personal accounts of their experiences. *Sistahs in College*, however, takes oral narrative methodology to a new level, not only in its riveting details, but also in the way that the narratives are organized to reveal distinctive information that is immediately transformative. Johnson-Bailey expertly uses italics to integrate extra-textual data that otherwise would be omitted or left to footnotes: introductions, conclusions, social, and historical material are interspersed throughout the narrative texts. As a result, readers are able to access the personal accounts of older women students with greater understanding than is ordinarily possible. The stories vary from woman to woman, and ultimately there emerges the kind of wisdom that is gained only through trials, difficulties, and successes. Intimate details of experiences in the home, classroom, and workplace suggest that factors internal and external to the university shape the course of a woman's life in ways that heretofore we could not determine.

In clear and abundant particulars women in this book unashamedly speak out about what it is like to go back to school later in life. They provide much needed information about a population almost forgotten and certainly not well documented—older African American women returning to college. Useful in numerous fields, this text revolutionizes the way we conceptualize women's lives and helps us to understand specific factors that contribute to their success in both undergraduate and graduate education.

In the very first chapter to *Sistahs in College* Johnson-Bailey describes her own personal simile for graduate school. It is incredibly striking and captures the essence of the "nontraditional" female student's feelings of isolation and "craziness." Not all share these feelings, but many of us will see ourselves and others in this book, a most important contribution to higher and continuing education.

It is not surprising that Juanita Johnson-Bailey would produce such a thought-provoking text. The insight that she brings to this work as well as the dignity with which she presents the narratives are characteristic of her unique scholarly approach to the study of women's lives. Readers will be challenged, informed, and intrigued by these personal narratives.

Gwendolyn Etter-Lewis
Professor and Graduate Director
Department of English
Western Michigan University

ACKNOWLEDGMENTS

I am indebted to my mother, Georgia, who taught me as a child to listen to the many layers of a person's story. Recognition is also owed to my father, William, who saw me begin this process but did not live to see me complete it. Through his usage and love of language, he instructed me about the nuances of discourse. And thanks also to my big sister Sheila, a great kindergarten teacher, who instilled in me, her first pupil, a love of learning. For these gifts, a love of stories, words, and learning, gleaned because of my family's tutelage, I am eternally grateful. Also, many thanks to Brandice, my daughter, and Marvin, my spouse, for their unwavering support and patience. They endured while I occasionally neglected them in pursuit of my dreams of schooling and writing.

My appreciation also to the seven women in this study who trusted me with their stories: Marcie, Sheila, Cathy, Lynda, Beth, Jean, and Faye. Four of them were given the names of my best women friends. Indeed I am indebted to both groups of women.

Additionally, I wish to recognize my former professors and present colleagues, Ronald M. Cervero and Patricia Bell-Scott, whose support and knowledge were essential to the conception and completion of my dissertation, which eventually resulted in *Sistahs in College*. A special thanks is also owed Lisa Baumgartner, my graduate assistant on this book, whose expertise as a proofreader, editor, and constant source of support was invaluable. And much appreciation to my graduate assistant Lynda Hanscome who manages and orders the saner part of my existence, the academic component. Finally, my appreciation to Krieger, Mary Roberts, and Elaine Rudd for their belief in the importance of this book and its subject matter.

ABOUT THE AUTHOR

Juanita Johnson-Bailey, Ed.D., is an associate professor of Adult Education and Women's Studies at The University of Georgia in Athens, Georgia. Her primary research interests include gender and race issues in education. She is the coeditor of *Flat-Footed Truths: Telling Black Women's Lives* (1998). Dr. Johnson-Bailey has written extensively about reentry Black women with articles most recently appearing in *Initiatives* and *Ms. Magazine*. She lives in Macon, Georgia, with her spouse, Marvin, daughter, Brandice, and mother, Georgia.

INTRODUCTION

What am I doing back in college at my age? Am I crazy? These questions frequently ran through my mind years past as I sat in college classes where I was often older than the teacher. Instead of doing the in-class assignment I would wonder why I felt so different, alone, stupid. In one class, a research course, I was attempting to decide on a topic for study, when I realized it would be fortuitous if this became a research interest since I spent so much time thinking about why I had returned to college. Surely there were other women like me, who were older than most of the typical students and who felt out of place. The answer was an easy one to find.

The number of women who enter college to work on degrees for the first time or those who are going back to complete degrees that they abandoned comprise the fastest growing segment of the college population. Currently they represent approximately 50 percent of all female college students. Yet this group and its concerns, which are different from those held by traditional students, are largely ignored by college administrators who schedule classes and events and establish hours of operation for the college business offices.

Most of the articles and books that I found did not discuss me, a woman of color, a Black woman who had returned to college after a twenty-year absence. Sure I had a lot in common with the White middle class women who were discussed as the usual reentry women, but there were other issues that kept coming up for me that were nowhere to be found. According to what I read, it was common to doubt your abilities, to feel less capable than younger students, and to feel guilty for abandoning your family. However, I was feeling something more. For instance, in this same research class the professor asked the students to give a simile to describe their school experiences. I dutifully committed my thoughts to paper. My classmates uttered platitudinous phrases such as, school was like a sea voyage—smooth sailing with a few rough days, or school is like a garden—full of flowers with a few weeds. My simile was quite different and described a painful story of an isolating and hostile schooling experience.

Maybe if I had not committed my feelings to paper I would not have felt compelled to share my thoughts. On that particular day, I could not mask my feelings. The class laughed, the teacher, who was one of my supporters, seemed confused, and I felt like a traitorous fool. Yet, that experience, more than any other, affirmed for me that returning to school had been different for me, a forty-year-old Black woman, than it had for many of my White counterparts. This awareness further isolated me from the class, but, luckily, I attended a research conference that same week and heard a Black woman presenter describe graduate school as being "like a radical mastectomy." There it was, another Black woman's truth. I was not crazy. Returning to school, while healing, reaffirming, challenging, and rewarding, in many ways mirrored my existence in society—it was often uncomfortable.

To find out if there were others like me and the presenter, I went in search of the schooling stories of other Black women. This book contains eight (including mine) narratives that were shared with me. Cathy, Beth, Jean, Marcie, Faye, Sheila, and Lynda traded tales of humor and pain with me. I asked them to tell me their most pleasant and painful memories of returning to school. The tales, laughter, and tears seemed to flood out of them as if they needed to tell and were just waiting for an audience. It was as if these reentry women were also wondering if they had been alone in their experiences.

There is much common ground among all women who return to school after twenty-five. Most are married with children according to national education statistics. Several major research studies have also shown that these women have tended to put others' needs ahead of their own. Now they are back in school and attempting to place this one need, school, center stage. Black women, however, are set apart from other reentry women by the low status they are ascribed in America in terms of who matters and who contributes most. The impact of living under such confines makes their experiences in college different from those of other nontraditional students.

The women I've written about come from varied backgrounds, age ranges, and experiences. All of the participants in this book reside in the South and most of their education occurred in the southeastern United States. However, their incidents are not bound by the parameters of the southern experience. When I have lectured and presented on my research nationally and internationally, I have heard similar stories from women in Chicago, San Diego, London (UK), Dallas, and Edmonton (AB). This confirmed for me that the eight women who tell their stories in this book are representative of everyday nontraditional Black women students. While regional and class variations certainly influenced the individual stories, it should be recognized that these women speak of a broader experience. In addition, recent studies conducted on similar groups of Black women in Illinois, Florida, California, New York, Texas, and Massachusetts echo corresponding accounts and resound with the same intense emotion.

In this book I call my collaborators sistahs and not sisters because the colloquial form connotes a more familial bond, especially among Black or African American women. Marcie, the youngest, is a thirty-four-year-old who lives with her parents and Lynda, the oldest, is a fifty-four-year-old with grown children and a grandchild. Most of them are first generation college students who are seeing the demands of academia through fresh eyes. Some of the more privileged women, Faye, Beth, and Marcie, have seen the major cities of the world, while others, Cathy and Lynda, have never been out of their home state. What they offer to us are their precious truths about returning to college, an environment that was intimidating for each of them in different ways and at other times an environment that was wonderfully stimulating.

I learn anew from their stories each time I read them. Marcie reminds me how privilege does not protect or guarantee your survival in college; Cathy lets me know that any obstacle that I may think I have is a minor one; and Lynda is always whispering that if you want it badly enough excuses are just that, excuses. Wit and wry wisdom skim the surface of each story. These sistahs are remarkable women. They have defied the odds to return to and complete school, battling nonsupportive families, meager finances, poor health, hostile classrooms, and mountains of self-doubt to find the wealth in each of their circumstances. Their stories provide a road map for overcoming that I return to again and again each time that I am lost or frightened.

CHAPTER 1

Juanita:
I've Seen the Sun
Come Up Many Nights

This story details why Juanita, the author of this book, returned to school at thirty-five to work on her graduate degree. It took three and one-half years for Juanita to complete her master's and doctoral degrees. She worked at a maddening pace and paid for it with her health. At times she would joke about working into the morning hours, saying that she would get her days and nights confused. Juanita's aggressive stance toward school reflects the attitude of many reentry women who rush headlong toward the goals that they feel they have deferred too long.

Prelude to Reentry

It was probably predestined that I'd go back to school again and again. School was a place that I loved. It was not always a reciprocal relationship, but I loved school. I attended a predominantly Black Catholic grade school in rural Alabama. I remember being free and feeling smart. My best memory of these days was epitomized by my role in the school Christmas pageant as Suzy Snowflake. I can still remember the little song, "Here comes Suzy Snowflake, dressed in a snow white gown, tap, tap, tapping, at your window pane, to tell you she's in town." But as I look back on it I was probably chosen because my mother was one of the few who could buy a gown for my role. Given the time period, the 1950s in the segregated South, it was likely that it was connected to my being a light-skinned, long-haired little child also. Back then, in that environment, light-skinned Blacks were considered superior, pretty, and preferable. I know now that I benefited from this, but I learned my lesson the hard way. In third grade a lighter skinned girl, Estelle Rogers, moved in and I took

5

my place with the other less desirables. But when you're little you think you're chosen to be Suzy Snowflake because you're smart.

Yet school for me was also a struggle to prove that I could. I don't remember a teacher ever telling me that I was smart. I just remember being told that I never worked up to my potential. It was near the end of my graduate program before a teacher ever told me that I was smart. I sat there as a forty-year-old woman fighting back tears of delight. School for some reason has always felt like an upstream swim.

I even ran away from first grade. The teacher disciplined me for not knowing all the words in the story. Although I read very well, I could not sound out the word "David." Sister Fidelis, my teacher, a very small woman that I towered over, took me to the board, wrote the word "David" on the board, placed her hand on the back of my head and pounded my head into the place where the word "David" was written. And when she left the room, I escaped. Actually, the word David had been introduced as a vocabulary word during the second week of school when I was out sick with the chicken pox.

Still I always figured that I was smart. I don't know why. I just suspected it. I loved school and met special people there. But there was one very special teacher who rescued me at a critical point in my schooling. Mrs. Marguerite Sherrill, my high school librarian, a petite woman with a too soft voice who wore her waist length braids bound about her head, would give me refuge in the back room of the library. I was the only Black girl in my high school class for all four years. She knew that it was hard for me. I was lonely, dateless, and intimidated most of the time. But it wasn't because my classmates weren't nice. I just had demons of inferiority.

My grades have always been above average, but I've never been the top student in any of my classes. I was always the one who tried hard and came in second, a 99, never a 100. But I loved school and it never took too much prodding to get me to study. School was the one place where I could thrive. And grades were a way of getting praise. So Mrs. Sherrill would make me do my work and tell me how I had to represent my race well. There would be days when she'd give me hugs for no reason. She was one of those well-meaning liberal White Southerners. I loved her and she helped put me on the road to wherever I will end up in life.

College was worse than high school. I had friends in high school: a Black set from the neighborhood and a White set from school. In grade school and in high school, I caught grief from my neighborhood friends who thought that I felt superior because I went to a Black Catholic grade school and then to a White Catholic high school. Many a day I was chased home and had to dodge rocks for some imaginary offense. For weeks after one of my White school friends visited me at home, I suffered.

However, in college I had neither set of friends. I was called an Oreo by the Black students who said I talked and acted White, as if such a thing actually existed. White students who were nice in class just ignored me after class. It seems that the idea of racial harmony had not arrived with me from the liberal Catholic school to my new Southern Baptist affiliated college. All the Black students stuck together and all the White students stuck together. I didn't fit in with the Black group and wasn't allowed in the White group.

But none of it mattered. I was in love. At seventeen I was foolishly in love. By the third day of school I spent all of my time with him. I would walk a mile across campus every morning to wake him up because he didn't like alarm clocks. It never occurred to me that I could sleep late since I didn't have any morning classes. My average was just a little above a B. I spent all of my time taking care of my boyfriend, even doing his homework. I had breakfast with him, lunch with him, and dinner with him. In between I'd squeeze my homework. Good thing he was a senior. That gave me two years to pull my average up and to save my academic scholarship. But I got the hell out of college two years after my boyfriend left by taking extra courses. Three years was long enough to attend college. I didn't fit in and I had no need to linger 'cause he was gone.

When I finished school I turned down a journalism scholarship to an Ivy League university that was offered through the national newspaper chain that I worked for and turned away overtures from my university's law school that was desperately looking for minority applicants.

This established a pattern for Juanita of putting other people and their needs before school and before herself. This phenomenon is common among reentry women. This self-sacrificing habit seems decidedly female and doesn't make for long-term happiness for the parties involved. Inevitably, women figure out that they are giving their dreams and opportunities away.

Reentering for Some of the Right Reasons

At first I thought it was important for me to earn this degree because of my Mama Dear. She always told me that education was the one thing that could not be taken from you and that I should get as much as possible. My mother had dropped out of school in the tenth grade. My dad finished high school in 1938 and tried to attend college. He had to drop out in his first year because his family could not afford the tuition. He later became a career soldier, serving twenty-two years in the Air Force. He spoke several languages and was a frustrated scholar. My parents put lots of emphasis on my report card, rewarding me monetarily for "A's." It was a given that I would go to college. I had to get as much education as I could get. My sister and I both went straight to college after high school.

I know so many older Black people who were brilliant and didn't have a chance to get an education. That probably weighed on my decision to return to school. I felt obligated to do it for all the Miss Sarahs and Miss Annie Maes in my life who were smarter than I could ever be, but who never got to go to school because it was inaccessible, it was not affordable, it was planting time, or they had to work.

I didn't feel that I had as much education as I could get and so I decided to pursue my doctorate. When my godfather heard that I was in school he said, "You always said that you were going to be a doctor. I guess you just didn't know what kind." He reminded me that when I was little my parents had bought me a toy nurse's kit that I had rejected saying, "I want to be a doctor, not a nurse." He reminded us that he had in turn bought me a doctor's kit that I accepted and later demolished with frequent play-play (*pretend*) examinations.

Another reason that I wanted to go to school was so that I would feel important. I felt that people would look at me differently if I had letters behind my name. My low self-esteem was part of my educational baggage. I realized during graduate school that having a doctorate was not going to change anything. I was going to be the same person and the people who would change towards me were people that I ought to watch out for or maybe stay away from. School did, however, cost me friends. There came a time when I had to choose between talking on the phone, visiting and going out with friends, or having any type of social life. School won out. So many of my friends got tired of being neglected. Others seemed to stay away from me, always explaining why they weren't in school. It was as if my being in school and following my dream made some of my friends uncomfortable, reminding them of their postponed dreams.

When I decided to go back to the state university, it was a painful and scary decision. I had been refused admission there to undergraduate school when I was seventeen. My high school principal told me that the state university was over its quota of minorities. He explained that the university was attempting a slow process of integration. It was a leap of faith for me to apply to this institution for a second time. Many people discouraged me because of the school's history. Desegregation had been a bitter battle. But my supervisors at work had been after me to go back to school. They kept telling me that they felt that I was in a dead-end job. These two women would tell me that I was meant for something better than the job I had.

With their encouragement I decided along with a friend to apply to school. We applied together. We had been inseparable at work. People referred to us as the Black half or the White half of the same person. I reasoned that school would be possible with a friend. She wanted to work on her doctorate and I would work on my master's. But I had always toyed with the idea that if I went back to school it would be for my doctorate and not a master's. I knew, from reading the small print of most graduate school catalogs, that you did not have to have a master's to get a doctorate. Actually, I knew that I could only endure higher ed one more time. I applied to the doctoral program. But I paid a price for going after this goal. Not only did my friend not join me in school, she never spoke to me again.

My undergraduate program had been so excruciating that I was afraid to go back to school. In some ways I think setting what seemed like an unrealistic goal was my way of preventing my reentry. My application was turned down. But surprisingly, I decided to fight, especially when I was told that it was because my undergraduate grade point average was too low. I had finished college in three years and with honors. The reason I was being refused admission to graduate school did not seem logical. Maybe it was arrogance, maybe old festering wounds, but I appealed the decision. And I received unconditional admission.

Because I started after fall quarter (my entry was delayed by one quarter while I was appealing) I started my program out of sequence and then found myself in the department's hardest doctoral level course with one of the department's toughest teachers. I struggled, but I prevailed. It was then that I first thought that maybe I could do this. However, smooth sailing was not in the cards. The university environment was not entirely accepting. I was lonely just as I had been in high school and in college. I would play this little game the first day of each class just to pass the time. It was called, "Who Will Sit Next to Me and When?" I'd always get to class early on the first day. I'd sit there as others filed in and took their seats. The game came about innocently. About the second or third quarter, I noticed that the only time students voluntarily sat next to me was when all the other seats were taken. I continued to play this sick little game for sanity's sake throughout my schooling. It was a way to laugh at the isolation. Finally, in my last quarter, a student sat next to me when there were other seats left. As it turned out, she was a university official who had been newly appointed to the president's Minority Affairs Committee. But I think she sat there more because of who she was as a person—an open and warm individual. We are still friends.

I didn't feel different in school because of my age although I knew that I stood out when I went outside of my department. Most of the students in my graduate program were nontraditional women also, so age was not a barrier for me in most of my classes. It was my race that made me stand out among others. When I entered my graduate program there was only one other Black student there. We depended on each other because we had to, but we would never have been friends outside of this setting. She would say to me that I was too different and "bourgeois" for her tastes. We formed our own study group, traded information often, proofread each other's work, and she even found scholarship money for me one quarter when I was in desperate financial need. She was a Northerner who thought that I was a backward Southerner, but we made it work because we didn't have a choice. I remember that the first bit of advice she gave me was not to come down here thinking that my Catholic school education made me as good as the "White folks" and that I shouldn't do my research on anything Black because I'd never get out of school. Although she was farther along in the program, I was capable of screening her advice. I knew that the only research that I wanted to do was on Black women.

For the most part, my problems in school were never with teachers. I found that it was a real dilemma dealing with other students. They questioned why I was there and wanted to know my GRE scores. The underlying question always seemed to be, "Are you an affirmative action placement?" For me it was like opening up old issues. When I was a first quarter freshman my advisor had insisted that I take remedial reading. When I refused, he told me that anyone who scored lower than 1000 on the SAT had to take remedial courses. Even when I explained that I had scored above this and even when he verified it, he still made me take remedial reading. Luckily, the remedial reading teacher placed me in regular classes after our first meeting. But being a minority in a predominantly White setting always made me feel that I was being suspected of something—usually it was inferiority.

I can only think of one instance where I had a real problem with a teacher. It was in a statistics class. I went in afraid as so many women do. Math and I have never been friends. I tried hard and I was so proud that the lowest grade that I made in the class was an "A–." When it came time for the final, I knew that I was home free. We had a take-home final that I spent four hours on and we had an in-class open-book final with no computations, just definitions. I spent three and one-half hours on it. I knew that I had done well. When my grades came, my husband and my daughter stood around as we had our little ceremonial grade opening. It usually went like this, "Oh, all "A's" again. How boring." Well I opened my grades and literally dropped to my knees crying. I had a "C" in statistics. I was devastated, not just because I felt that I had been graded unfairly, but because I somehow thought that I would go all the way through school with a 4.0 grade point average on a 4.0 grading scale. I've since abandoned that unrealistic notion.

The first person I called was my classmate Clarice. She and I were the only older women in the class and we had bonded because of this commonality. We had actually gone to the same college as undergraduates but had never known each other. Things were so segregated then that we would not have been friends. I had helped her all quarter and I sort of knew that she had borrowed my work several times without my permission. She resisted telling me what grade she had made. I had scored higher than she had on each assignment and test and so I just knew that she had failed also. After several telephone conversations she admitted reluctantly that she had earned a "B." She encouraged me to accept the "C" quietly. Thank goodness my major professor helped me to fight it and helped to write an appeal.

It was Christmas week and I couldn't reach my statistics professor. His department head defended him by saying that he would be happy to look at my final. I remember telling him that he would have to look at mine and everyone else's in order to rule out subjectivity. Several weeks into my appeal, I returned home to find a very clipped message on my home answering machine, "Everything you said was accurate. Your grade has been changed." I was never told why I received the "C" and I was never told why the grade was changed. But at that time something inside of me broke. I couldn't pretend any longer that everything was fair.

As so many reentry women do, Juanita struggled with doubt. What had she done wrong in the class? How was it her fault? But as so many reentry women claim, intuitively she knew all along that there were problems. Quite often nontraditional women students are hardworking and driven. They are not going to college because it is expected but because they want to go. As serious-minded students who are their teachers' age peers, they often approach their professors with surprising deference but with high expectations.

I knew that I wasn't the teacher's favorite pupil. I knew that I had asked so many questions, but I was paying for my education this time, out of my own pocket. I wasn't on scholarship. My parents weren't paying. It wasn't enough for me to pass. I wanted to understand. I guess I bothered him. On some level, I had sensed that he wasn't fair. But the idea of fairness is a childish concept. So I ignored it. He told jokes about how having women or athletes in classes lowered the Z score of test groups. But I tuned that out. Somehow I think I might have even pretended to laugh. A lesbian friend of mine had warned me that he didn't like her because she was out of the closet and different and that he liked his women students passive. Still I thought that she couldn't possibly mean that I was doing anything wrong. I wasn't being assertive, just attentive.

Baptism by Fire

I think people feel that Black women can take care of themselves. I remember professors saying that they didn't worry about me because I could take care of myself. So they didn't lead me to water the way they did for other students.

Part of the fault though was mine. I had to learn to accept help. My major professor, Ron, would ask me if I needed help and I would tell him no. I just wasn't used to asking for and getting help from White men. All the saviors in my life had been Black women. So I would lie to him and tell him that I was okay when I was not. But I reasoned that I was supposed to be strong and that this situation suited us both. Since I commuted to campus and didn't spend a lot of time on campus, I could get away with this lie. At home, I was crying and drowning.

During a class activity, it finally hit me that my experiences in graduate school were different. The teacher had asked that we write down a metaphor or a simile for our graduate school experiences. My answer skewed all the other answers. My classmates said that school was like a garden, some weeds but mostly flowers or that school was like an ocean voyage, mostly smooth seas with occasional rough waters. I said that school was like skipping barefoot through broken glass, mostly large chunks of glass with a few small pieces here and there. My answer angered the class and hurt my professor, who had truly treated me fairly. But it was my truth. School was different for me than it was for my counterparts. I would have thought I was crazy too by everyone's reaction had I not gone to a conference the following week and heard a Black woman speak who had just finished her graduate studies. She said that graduate school was like a radical mastectomy. I knew that I was not crazy. She said that college was challenging for nontraditional students but that adding the layer of woman and race to the mix could make for a traumatic experience.

I'm sure that if I had learned to keep my mouth shut, I would have had a more positive experience. I guess I just didn't know my place. I always thought that I had something meaningful to say. And I don't have to guess whether or not I angered my peers. They told me, especially near the end of my studies when we would have to evaluate each other's research. I was doing my work on what happens to older nontraditional Black women when they return to college. Knowing that my experiences were different made me want to find out how other Black women were doing in their school journeys. A few of my classmates would tell me too that my work was not relevant, that its scope was too small, and that no one would be interested. I think their comments made me work harder and my work better. I'd resist their comments and counter with arguments and sharp words. But I'd curse and process it all over again on the way home. It didn't stop me though. I was afraid to stop. If I stopped, I wouldn't get going again—ever.

On a typical day I get up at 6 a.m. and get to work around 8 a.m. I had a daily forty-mile commute to work. I would do my work and leave around 3 p.m. for the one hundred-mile commute to school. In all, I averaged 1,000 miles a week. To fit school into my life, I had to work a flexible schedule. I'd work through my lunch break in order to leave at 3 p.m. three days a week. Class lasted from 4:30 to 9:30 p.m. Then I'd drive the one hundred miles home. If I had homework or a paper, I'd stay up all night or at least until the sun came up signaling morning. Then I might catch a quick twenty minute nap and drag into work. I didn't sleep much. It was only three days a week though and if there were no pressing assignments I'd come in from work and go straight to bed. On weekends I slept the sleep of the dead. My car was a pig sty because I ate most of my meals there, changed clothes there, and sometimes caught a quick nap in the parking lot. The only time it got really bad was when I had a 9 a.m. class. That meant my day would start at 5 a.m. and that my schedule would be inverted, ending with a work day.

Finding My Way to My Dreams

Some of the ways in which Black reentry women differed from other reentry women was in their desire to continue working while enrolled in school. For many of them, this meant that they attended college on a part-time basis. For others, it meant an impossible life of full-time employment, school, and family responsibilities. After a while, all areas suffered from benign neglect.

I came back to school with the intention of opening up new opportunities. I knew that my life wasn't right and I thought that maybe I'd have to start out again on my own to fix it. I envied my husband's life. He had pursued all of his dreams. He had his own business and I had supported him emotionally. I felt that it was now my turn. I felt entitled to a terminal degree before I struck out on my own. What I realized while in school was that I had willingly sacrificed my life to my spouse and to my child, but that they had not asked me to do this. It seemed like what I was supposed to do.

I had met my husband when I was seventeen. He was my first real boyfriend. I sort of gave my life away. Once I got to graduate school, I realized that I was bored with the life I had created for myself. At the time I went back to school my life consisted of work, child care, housework, and going to sporting events, basketball and football, to watch my spouse referee. I wouldn't know either team at the sporting events, but I didn't have any hobbies, so I tried to enjoy his hobby. Graduate school made me realize that I needed to reclaim my life. There was nothing wrong with my husband. There was something wrong with me. I'd voluntarily and forcibly given my dreams away. My spouse had resisted, but I had insisted.

From the time I finished college and got married, my husband had encouraged me to go back to school and to pursue my doctorate. He was more positive than anyone else. But I was so scared and locked into my role as mother and wife that I couldn't hear him. It was only maturity and the thought of going to a school with a buddy that influenced my decision to try school. When I was refused admission, he couldn't convince me to appeal the decision. It was a sorority sister of mine who had also been refused admission to the same college who told me not to take it personally. She had been denied admission to this same school and she was currently receiving her third degree from the university. I guess it was just important for me to know that someone else had been through the same thing and had survived.

Also, I was afraid of school. It had never been a completely safe place. When I went back to school my husband cooked all the meals, woke me every morning, ironed my clothes for school, and answered my screams in the early morning hours when the computer would go berserk. He'd grumble and bump into furniture, but he'd always get up and fix the computer or the printer.

It was a different story with my daughter. She gave me mixed messages. She hated that school took me away from her. That's normal. School took me away from her basketball games and school events. And when I was home I was always studying or sleeping. In retrospect, I wish I had not taken three and sometimes four courses some quarters or I wish that I had not worked full-time. It got so bad that if anyone from school called, she tried to distract me from my conversation. It was her way of saying that, "The little time when you are home, school should not intrude." She jealously guarded our time together. Going back to school definitely damaged our relationship. But when is it a good time for a mother to return to school? If you go back to school when they are young, they will feel abandoned. If you go back to school when they are older they will be resentful and capable of acting out their resentments. I've had friends tell me stories of children erasing computer disks or moving their assignments. I don't think it's malicious. I just think children are programmed to expect that mothers are there to fulfill all of their needs.

I've tried to make it better and to let my example encourage her to pursue an education. Whenever something exciting is going on, I bring her to campus. On the rare occasions when I've had Black women professors, I made certain that she met them. They intuitively knew the score and were always kind to her. She felt so special. One of them even gave her an autographed copy of a book she had written. I've caught her showing it to her friends and so I know she's proud of me and the people I get to meet. But that is balanced against her not having her mother full-time like her friends who don't have moms in school or at work. Still, she would bring me cups of tea and give me the most wonderful massages for my computer weary shoulders.

None of that seems to matter now. Just being in school has changed me. It's like I'm charged up and I'm finding my way at last. And I know now that there are other dreams that I'm going after next. I want to write and I want to do research about women like me. I am capable.

Juanita's story is quite typical. Every day women go back to school in hopes of changing their world. School was initially difficult. Since she had neglected her health, the new schedule took its toll on her body. The 1,000 mile per week commute exacerbated her old spinal injury. After a year of driving, she dropped out of school for three quarters to have surgery. When she returned, she got her master's degree just in case her health did not hold out through her doctoral program. It did. And she graduated with her master's and her doctorate after three and one-half years. Juanita now teaches in a graduate education program and has many reentry women as students. She jokes with them when they talk to her about fears and she trades stories with them about the number of irrational fears she had when she was in their shoes. Mostly she solicits their stories about their plans for their lives after education. Juanita still believes that giving voice to dreams and then sharing them with others who are supportive are the first steps in realizing them. She knows that her life's path had many digressions just so that she can now sit and listen with an understanding ear.

CHAPTER 2

Cathy:
The Wrong Side of the Tank

This story shows so much pain and poverty it seems at times surreal. The title comes from a childhood remembrance of an army tank that patrolled Cathy's neighborhood in the days following Martin Luther King Jr.'s assassination. This pivotal point in her life made her aware of the differences that governed the lives of Blacks and Whites. Cathy began to look around at her world with a more critical eye. One of her realizations was that her education was separate and unequal. This awareness created a sadness that stymied her childhood quest to achieve in school but has transformed into an adult's understanding that drives her need to achieve. Cathy is desperate to get her degree. Her story reminds each of us that deferred dreams are waiting for us to claim them. When we do, it seems that we will pay any price to finally make them come true.

Introduction

Cathy is a petite thirty-nine-year-old Black woman who exudes joy. She lives in a cramped two bedroom apartment with her five-year-old daughter and eleven-year-old son. Her "place" is located in a cul de sac in Bird City, a government housing project so nicknamed because the streets have names such as Wren, Dove, and Crane. With quick, energetic, and constant movements, her smile, which is wide and sincere, accompanies constant gestures and intense eye contact.

When I arrived to pick her up on a Saturday afternoon in February, Cathy was dressed in pale blue sweat pants, an outdated frayed orange and yellow plaid wool coat that was two sizes too small, and a fluorescent yellow skull cap that covered her eyebrows and ears. Her bizarre dress belied her sharp wit and brilliant conversational style. Cathy's positive attitude seemed to ignore her desolate surroundings and this zest carried over to her conversations about school.

Despite a history of good grades in elementary and high school, she was hesitant to enter college. In her early thirties, Cathy says she feels old when she's at school. High school coincided with the beginning of integration and Cathy vividly remembers being ridiculed by White teachers and students. She has residual feelings of inadequacy that she attributes to those traumatic times. It took much encouragement by a friend who was also enrolled in college to convince Cathy to take a chance on herself. This girlfriend persuaded her by constantly reminding her of how smart Cathy had been when they were in school together.

Cathy has been enrolled in a nursing program at a community college for a year. Although she is an honors student, she recently decided to change her major to elementary education because she believes that the nursing program is unfair to Blacks and because she does not want to "endure" the program.

Framing her adult schooling were memories of childhood experiences. She mentioned her initial experiences often as she grappled with describing how school was fitting into her adult life. Although Cathy maintained that the disturbing events which occurred in her grade school and high school years were not connected to the present, it seemed more a wishful thought than a reality in which she believed.

Unequally Separate

I lived through the era of segregation. So I remember too well how much it influenced me, especially in the way I feel about my school days. In the early grades, I had no idea that there were differences between the way Blacks and Whites lived. But things were happening in my community and in home life. Back then the newspaper had a "colored" section. It seemed that all the news in the colored section was bad. Not that we didn't have our own clubs and organizations, but then hard things were happening in the world. I also remember my mother taking me four blocks away from where she was spending her money, to go the "colored only" restroom. Yet we were lucky. I watched TV and I know that elsewhere people were dying.

In our city we had a mayor who placed a 6:00 p.m. curfew on the city. It was supposedly for White and Black neighborhoods, but it was racial. He purchased a tank and rode around in Black neighborhoods only. It was his intention to intimidate people. I was a little girl, around nine years old, but I remember him riding through our neighborhood when I was playing in the yard with a friend. Even though we were just children, the police told us to get back on the porch. But it was warm and we were playing in the yard the way children are supposed to play on warm summer days.

In spite of all of this, school was still fun. Achieving is the most fun I've ever had—being able to learn new things. My most pleasant memory of school was being involved in a little small play where I was Miriam of the Biblical story of Moses. My mother couldn't come because she had to work, but my father, who never lived with us, agreed to come. I felt kind of special. But in subsequent years, my father and I have never been really close.

I worked hard in the early part of school. During high school I had spring fever—hormonal uproar. I let a few subjects slide. Overall I finished with a 2.3. It wasn't that I couldn't do it. I just got lazy, rebellious, carefree. It was almost over. Why work?

Cathy's age puts her in the unique position of having been a product of both segregated and newly integrated school environments. Like many Black reentry women in their thirties and forties, she recalls her days of inequality with fondness because in this sheltered world she felt safe and smart. The days of difference were difficult for her and served as a marker for her educational and life narrative. Her statements about this period are terse and pain-ridden.

Some teachers would talk to you in such tones. The words did not matter. They would talk down to you. It was as if they knew that your background was lacking—your parents were uneducated and you were ignorant. But that wasn't the case. I remember how difficult it was to look in the teacher's eyes and ask a question. I feared asking a dumb question. When I did ask a question, it was out of sheer necessity, and I'd hear, "Well, you should know this," or "Why are you asking me this?" The kids would snicker and the teacher would not answer. And my ego would slouch even further.

I witnessed a lot of rifts between classmates. Once one of my Black friends chased a White girl all around the room. I could see the fear in both girls' eyes. I guess everyone was feeling a certain amount of pain. I know Black people were hurting long before King ever talked to the world about all the injustices. When the schools integrated, the kids, Black and White alike, came with harsh feelings and severe hostilities that grown people encouraged.

In addition to the period being painful, Cathy thinks that the disparity of her schooling was evident. According to her, the new formerly all-White schools had varieties of equipment and books that she had never seen before.

My schools did not prepare me adequately even though I maintained good grades. It was hard for me. When the schools integrated the White kids who came from "more equal" institutions did better. It appeared easier for them. Yet I believe that attending all Black public schools was a good experience in a way because it gave me a sense of identity. I didn't feel different.

Often when discussing decisions made in youth, there seems to be regret in Cathy's voice. The same seems true for so many reentry women. Phrases like, "If I only had known then what I know now," or "Hindsight is twenty-twenty, but real life vision is blurry," are common refrains. The thirties and forties are not only years for reflecting on what you could have done differently, but seemingly for women these years are times for finishing or beginning those tasks that can still be accomplished.

Revisiting Math and Science Demons

When I was in high school, I had the opportunity to go to Upward Bound. But no. I could kick myself now for thinking, "No. I don't want to go. I'm working. I'm working making nothing." Then came children, marriage, and divorce. Now I want to secure more of a future for my children. I've missed so many opportunities. I want to do better and obtaining a higher level of education will be my ticket.

Making the final decision to go to school was hard and I didn't make it alone. I was influenced by a friend that I kept running into at the laundromat. She said, "Cathy you were so smart. Did you go to school?" And I would say, "Nah." And she would tell me about the local community college and tell me that I should go. Every time I'd see her, she'd tell me this. She'd hound me about going back to school. And it got so that I stopped going to the laundromat.

When I made the decision to go to college, I was so afraid. The counselor will tell you the many times I called her at home and said, "Uh, uh, uh, I can't do this." She would say, "Yes you can." I was coming up with all types of excuses. I was afraid. The fear of failure. It's been too long. I won't fit. I kept going back and forth. When I finally made the decision to go, I think it was the best decision I could have made. I was staying at home. I was on the system—Welfare. I had low self-esteem. I'd had good jobs in the past. I didn't want to sling hamburgers. And so I said, "Well, let me see how I can use this system to help myself so that I can get off Welfare."

The school sent me an application to complete for the minority Summer Enrichment Program. I didn't just send it back in the mail. I completed it, signed it, and took it out there the same day. But I didn't get in. There were no more spaces. I was crushed. They were trying to gear it towards the traditional student. I said to myself, "I'm the one who needs the little extra boost, the incentive and the help." And so every other day I would call the counselor for the program. They (the school officials) had never seen my face, but they knew me well. I was so determined to get out there. I would call every other day and say, "Do you have a space available—maybe somebody is sick—maybe somebody decided to go somewhere else?" And so finally, maybe about a week before the class was supposed to start, they sent me a letter. I got in. Later I found out that no one dropped. They had fifty slots open and they made it fifty-one because the secretary said listen, "You have got to get this Cathy in here, into this class."

Cathy has dealt with many rejections in her lifetime. It didn't embarrass her to let the school officials know how much she wanted to gain admission into their program. According to her, the worst that could happen would be that they'll just keep saying no. Past ordeals had taught her tenacity. She felt that she had nothing to lose and everything to gain. A wealth of life experiences from which to draw solace and guidance is one factor that sets reentry women students apart from younger women students.

I was so happy to get in. It was fantastic. I said, "Thank God," because I knew I needed it. I needed that Summer program. I didn't know if my nerves could last until September. This would be something to get me reacquainted with school.

I did things in that program that I had never done before. We went to museums and we got a chance to go to the Martin Luther King Center. It was real. We went on a tour of his house. I saw Coretta Scott King. I never had the money to go to those places.

After the Summer program I wanted to bail out. The counselor said, "No, you're not. Not as many times as you bugged us. You are staying in." And so everything worked out.

My life since I came back to school has been a roller-coaster ride. At first I felt a sense of intimidation, not knowing if I could measure up. There were a lot of insecurities. The first day there I looked around. I always sit up front in the middle of the T. And I could feel their eyes. That's my inferiority complex. I felt like everyone was looking at me like, "What is she doing?" I was the oldest. They used to call me mother, the mother hen. I had this feeling from the kids that I didn't belong. Then they started seeing that I was the one who was the first to ask questions. I was the one, you know, who was bringing in the homework and just really trying, trying, to do my best. I guess my age had its benefits. I was serious 'cause I had been through a lot of things. Age worked to my advantage. Before it was over with, I had won their respect. It was a good feeling.

During her second week of school, Cathy's car stopped working and she could not afford to repair it or to buy a new one. But she was already hooked on school and did not let her transportation problems deter her. She started commuting by bus.

I will never forget this one incident. I had missed the bus 'cause it would come so early. I had to get up—the children and everything. I just missed the bus. I was determined to get to school. My class was at 10:00 in the morning. It was 8:00 a.m. so I decided to walk. I said from where I live to the college is no problem until I started walking. It was raining and I fell. I got soaked. I looked back. I could see my house. I looked the other way and I couldn't see the college. But I was determined to go. I had to go. I walked up the street, slish, slosh, slish, slosh. I didn't want to miss, not just 'cause I had to walk. I wasn't sick. The children weren't sick and I didn't want to miss school. I was determined to get there. I had to get there. My hair shriveled. It's a good eight miles. It costs about $4.00 to get there in a cab.

Cathy made it to school that day and every day thereafter. She talks readily of good times and negative experiences. Overall, it is harder than she imagined and more empowering than she expected.

There have been some hilarious times when I've had to stop and laugh at myself. I've shied away from math like many women. I eventually took the hard math course, the one designed to prepare me for nursing. There was one problem that still tickles me. The workbook said Ms. Doe has been prescribed .5 milliliter of a drug and your solution stock is 100 percent. How do you dilute it? I said to myself, "Oops! This lady is dead." It had been so long since I took math that I just didn't get it. Though I was frightened, I learned to master it. Things did start coming back to me and I made an "A" in the class. It's a different type of math, doing equations, quadrants, linears. So I said "Let me get some remediation," even though I had been exempted from Development Studies because I made a passing score on my college preparatory exam. You have to take the college preparatory exam if you have been out of school for over ten years or longer or if you have never been to college. You have to pass the exam's three parts. Taking extra courses just to make sure you understand seems like a common thing for older students to do. We want to be sure we can keep up. I have one friend who goes to school out here. She is taking some developmental studies, not because she wasn't exempted. She feels that she just needs to better prepare herself.

When asked to describe school, Cathy said it was like a roller-coaster ride, full of ups and downs. Here are some moments that she identifies as memorable ones on her reentry ride.

In my first year at the college I was nominated by my English 101 teacher for the honors program. And that first day I was the only little Black woman in there and the oldest again. And I called my counselor that night and said, "I'm leaving this." I felt like I had the weight of the rest of the Blacks at the college on my shoulders. I'm the only Black in the class. That old inferiority complex had me asking, "Can I do this?" I was afraid to fail. I would rather bail. I was so intimidated. Let me tell you what I discovered. Those kids in those classes don't know anymore than you do. If they are in the class it's for the same reason I'm there. Someone nominated them just like they nominated me. Still I felt it was all on me. I pulled a B out of the class. It felt good when I was one of the participants to walk up on the honors stage.

Some things do get me down. I was in a sociology class and the students were talking about Welfare recipients and homeless people. I didn't know that real people felt that way about people like me. You see people on talk shows saying cruel things about how poor and homeless people are in their circumstances because they prefer those conditions. Who wants to be homeless? To me that is ludicrous. I tried to respond in class. Then they asked me questions like, "Why don't they go on birth control and stop having babies? We're taxpayers." Apparently they don't know that things sometimes don't happen the way people plan. No one plans to be poor.

On one of my very first days of class, an instructor said, "Open your book to chapter four. If you don't know the first three chapters then you don't need to be in this class." It had been such a long time since I dealt with algebra. I skimmed through the three chapters. And the first chapter was okay, but when I saw those algebraic equations. I said, "Oh man I don't know this." The teacher was taking the class so fast. It was hard for me to learn it that fast. I didn't understand it like I should have. I withdrew and took remedial math for a refresher. Later I made an A for that course. The next time I take a math course I'll be more prepared.

I didn't feel prepared for anatomy and physiology either. It was a two-part class—lab and lecture. Everyone has problems with it unless you have the background for it. This course is the moneymaker for the college since it has such a large failure rate. Everyone knows that a third of the students in each class don't complete the course and the majority of those who remain won't make a passing grade. The average student has to take it three times in order to pass. Mostly the people who do well have private school backgrounds where they took anatomy and physiology in high school.

I didn't understand all the chemistry. I didn't take chemistry in high school. And so I got a lot of self-help books. Maybe I needed more books and more time. But for whatever reason I didn't get it. Instead of slowing down, the class sped up. I didn't feel mentally ready. I couldn't absorb that much. It took me so long just to understand one chapter. Mainly it was the terminology, the medical language. I had to look up every few words because I wanted to know what they meant and I wanted to be able to pronounce them. It slowed me down. It was very difficult.

I tried to talk to the teacher. He told me that there was no substitute for three or four hours of studying per day. At first I thought he was being smart. Then I thought about it. He was making all kinds of assumptions about me. Now I hadn't been studying that much because I can't study at home. It's so comfortable there and then there are the dishes. There is food. There's the telephone. I come to school early in the morning to study and study anywhere else that I find quiet. My schedule makes it hard to have four straight hours. Maybe he was telling the truth. I am deficient.

Of course the teacher didn't seem at all interested in me. He assumed that

I was not studying adequately. He dismissed me. I tried to ask him if he felt that I should take remedial courses. But he said that we were just touching the surface. But everything I saw was a chemical formula. The molecular structures looked foreign. And I didn't understand about conservation and reduction. I could see the definition but I didn't understand about adding and removing the water.

There is a test coming up and the teacher told me to wait until after the test to decide about staying in the class. I made a 70 on the first test and he thought that it was a good grade. I didn't think it was acceptable. Of course I'd take that over an "F." But there was no leeway.

The counselor wanted me to hang in there. I gave it serious thought and decided to pull out. It's not the first time I've done that. But each time that I have made that decision it has worked best for me. I dropped a psychology course because my teacher was in another world. And when I took it from a different instructor I made an "A." Well I had a feeling, intuition, something inside, a knowledge within myself. I knew I didn't understand the test. I have no regrets. I dropped the class because I didn't feel prepared. Even though I made a 70 on the test, it was like walking along a ledge. I didn't even take the second test. Actually there were two tests on the same day, the regular test and the lab exam. The class test was going to cover twelve chapters. A lot of students took the second test and failed it miserably. And everyone I talked to asked me had I dropped the course. If they didn't fail the lecture, they failed the lab part.

Cathy dropped the course. She said that she had to follow her heart. Respecting your inner voice seems to be a common trait among the reentry women.

Maybe I would be better qualified in elementary education. A girlfriend told me that I looked like a teacher. It shocked me. She said that she would let me teach any of her six children but that if she saw me in her hospital room as a nurse she said she'd have to ring for help. I've had the opportunity to tutor a fellow classmate and I was uplifted. I had a sense of pride and satisfaction in helping others learn. I've always taught, whether it's working with my children at home or working with neighbors. There are other nursing programs. But I have transportation problems. I'm not closing the door on it. I want to get better prepared—to take biology and chemistry. I don't want a week to learn 206 bones inside and out. It may take me longer. I would rather be qualified. Black women have to be 105 percent qualified anyway in order to succeed in the long run.

There have been really good experiences. I had a poem published in the school magazine. It was hard for me to conceive that something that I had written was good enough to be seen by anyone else. I went on to write short stories and then essays. I won first place in a Minority Student Enrichment

Program. You know the one that I begged to get in to. Now after a year, I feel more confident about trying new things.

The new confidence in the school setting is fragile. Yet, it is encased in an adult's understanding that school is a business. There are rules and ways of succeeding. Cathy quickly applies previously learned life lessons to this environment.

The first day of class before the bell, I go to meet the instructor to find out their office hours. It's not necessarily brown nosing but to try to get an impression of them. Hopefully, it gives them a positive impression of me. It's also a good opportunity to ask questions about the class. I've gotten insider information this way—about books and about any additional aids I might need to buy. I don't hesitate to ask for help.

I get to class early. I look on my left and say, "Hello, my name is Cathy. What's your name? And if you don't mind could we exchange numbers." I made it a rule of thumb to do this in every class.

Riding the Roller Coaster

My children are so proud of me. I often hear them tell their friends, "You know that my Mama goes to college." A lot of mothers around the neighborhood, for whatever reason, don't do anything. Now more and more mothers are going back to school. Some went back, I guess, because they saw me and realized that anyone could do it. Now there's a lot of media attention being given to women on Welfare who go back to school. The Housing Authority, who manages the housing project where I live, promotes entrepreneurship, GED completion programs, and community college programs. First it was a neighbor who went to the community school. Then I enrolled. Now there are two more women from my area who have started classes.

I think maybe I'm becoming a role model. The woman that I ride with just started school. She's a little older and she was very concerned. She was intimidated and overwhelmed by the amount of information and the new life that she was experiencing. Looking at her was like looking at a frightened chicken running around. I had to stop her and unruffle her feathers. She had actually started talking about dropping out of school. I told her, "You just got in. You're not going anywhere."

Cathy's pride in succeeding is short-lived. According to her it's always something. Every time she thinks it's smooth sailing something happens. Her greatest joy in school, enrolling in an honors program, was clouded in controversy.

When I went to sign up for my first honors class, I was so proud. Not many students get this opportunity, especially Blacks. You get selected for these classes by having high standardized test scores or you have to be recommended by a professor. I had been recommended by my English teacher and it was a big deal for me. So there I was standing in the honors line. I was aware that I was the only Black and that I was surrounded by blue-eyed, blonde haired young girls, cheerleader types. And just as this realization hit me, a professor who was supervising the line came and stood next to me, looked directly at me, and announced that if there was anyone in the honors line that was not invited into the program, they should move to the other line. Well I didn't move. As I approached the registration desk, he took his place at the table. I watched him intensely after he made the announcement. He did the paperwork for several young women in front of me without question. When it was my turn, he asked, "Were you invited into the honors program? Do you have an invitation letter from a faculty member?" As I pulled the letter from my purse he processed my papers, placing the honors sticker on my registration card. He refused to look at my letter. I insisted. For that one moment it felt good. But it ticked me off. And it made me wonder again about everything.

I'd like to think that it's not as bad as it used to be when I was a little girl. I know individuals have their old gripes and prejudices on both sides, Blacks and Whites. But there have been several teachers, and I can't prove it, but there are advisors at my school that advise and treat Black students differently. Many are advised right out of school during their first quarter. They are told to take full loads, three and four courses. A lot of these people have been out of school for a while—twenty years or more—and they are easily discouraged because this is a brand new experience. A lot of them are the first ones in their family to attend college, just like me. And so we advise each other. We have to stick together because Black flight is occurring at my school. Black students are leaving in significant numbers. The numbers are getting smaller and smaller.

I'm a very different student now than when I first entered. The counselor at my college has taught me to hang in there. I'm more confident, committed, determined, very serious. Even though some people say you should never say never, there comes a time when you realize that you have potential and that you are only allotted so many days on this earth. I know this. I have already waited too long.

Cathy, like the majority of women of color and poor women who return to college, attends a community college. This point of entry has a higher drop-out rate than traditional four-year institutions; but one advantage to attending a community college is that there are often remedial programs and more flexible class schedules. Such benefits are important to Cathy because she has been out of school so long that many terms and behaviors that are commonplace to traditional-age students are foreign to her. Playing catch-up is particularly important in the sciences and mathematics for many returning women students. In addition, Cathy's single parent status necessitated that she have some flexibility in when she attended classes.

Cathy's description of school as a roller-coaster ride is indicative of the events she described as her day-to-day school life. But she smiles through it all and says that she just won't quit. This sense of now or never seems particular to women who are finally in school after a delay. The ability to take the good with the bad and to keep it all in perspective is a benefit of the wisdom that comes with experience. For Cathy, it seems to be an advantage that is buckling her safely into that roller-coaster seat.

CHAPTER 3

Marcie:
Without a Pot,
Without a Window

What do you do when you believe in yourself, but no one else does? This is Marcie's dilemma, a woman who has fought for the last nine years in an on-again-off-again battle to obtain her undergraduate degree. She comes from a family of high achievers. Her three siblings and parents all have advanced degrees, while Marcie is still trying to obtain her undergraduate degree. Will she do it this time after dropping out so many times before? It is a question she often asks herself and unfortunately one that she is asked too often by family and friends. Marcie has a story of perseverance to teach anyone who will listen.

Introduction

Marcie is a thirty-four-year-old Black woman whose appearance is at once commanding and elegant. She's tall, five feet eleven inches, fashionably slim, and posture perfect. With a quick wit, her face lights up often with a wide smile followed inevitably by a boisterous laugh. Her skin is smoky black and her eyes narrow and expressive. To look at her polished veneer, you'd never guess the pain.

When Marcie and I first met to discuss her experiences as a nontraditional college student, she was in what she hoped would be her final year of school. In the very formal and refined dining room of her parents' home, we sat for several hours sharing gourmet coffee, Danish cookies, and painful stories of struggling through college.

It was the wall of about fifty photos standing guard behind us that set a disturbing context for our talk. There were pictures of her father, a retired army officer, with various dignitaries, and several of his certificates and commendations.

One picture in particular stood out. It was the framed cover of a national maga-zine and it featured her brother at his Ivy League medical school graduation amidst a sea of White faces. As she noticed my interest, she explained about the wall of accomplishments. She has three younger siblings: a brother, the doctor; a brother, the doctor and lawyer; and a sister, the dentist. And she is the oldest and the only child in this family, where credentials clearly matter, who has not yet finished college.

Droppin' Out and Dropping Back Again

As a traditional college coed Marcie attended two historically Black colleges. Now, as an older returning student she has tried two White schools and has now returned to one of her former Black institutions. In Marcie's opinion her college career has had more spins than a ferris wheel ride. According to her, she's just trying to make a way out of no way. She understands how school works. Every-one in her family does school well. And the track record of family school suc-cesses encompasses her conversation as she explains about her early schooling and her reentry experiences. She begins her story with her parents credo about her responsibilities regarding school.

Your job was to go to school and get good grades. I think that that's the way we, my generation, were raised. I'm a military brat. So it was Daddy out there working and Mommy holding down the home front and her job. Your part in this, in this puzzle, is to go to school. Get up every morning and go to school to get what they've got. It was a responsibility and I think that's part of why I went back. I felt that I had shirked a responsibility.

My Dad is number twelve of twelve children and the only one to receive a college degree. Actually, he is the only one to finish high school. He went to the Army. Came out and went to school on the GI Bill. Then back into the service as an officer. My mother returned to school as a continuing ed student during my father's second tour in Viet Nam with four children in tow and she handled it. She was busting grades. She was on the plan, working one semester and going to school the next. So I'm a second generation continuing ed stu-dent. You think that from one generation to the next things should progress and get better and so there's a little bit of "Umph umph umph" with me and my parents. They see me as a projection of them. I have two brothers that are doctors, and a sister who is a dentist. One of my brothers has a law degree as well but doesn't practice law. My mother says, "You were the smartest of all my children. Why are you here? You should have letters behind your name." How does a parent deal with that disappointment in such a way that you don't estrange your child or have that child spiraling in their own form of psychosis. But if it doesn't happen, Does that mean that it's no longer your child?

Going to school was my job and I didn't get the promotion. Didn't earn it. I was supposed to go to school for four years and then move on because there were other children behind me who were due to go to school. Four years of school and I had changed my major two or three times and didn't have a degree. But my time was up, so I got a job. I left school and got a job.

Marcie was resigned to walking the path which she had chosen. She was eight years into a comfortable job in the telecommunications industry when she had a revelation as to what her life without college would entail. A chance encounter with a senior employee became a turning point for her.

And I had been at this job coming up on eight years and there was this little old lady, wearing her little senior service pin, saying that she needed me to look at this catalog 'cause we need to choose your ten-year gift. My mouth was open. I was like, I have been here that long and I'm doing the same thing. Now I'm looking at a catalog and I'm debating the merits of a Cross pen set with the company logo and a mug or a plate with 14-karat gold trim to hang on a wall. I'm like, "I can't do this." You know every once in a while there are things in your life that hit you. It says you can't do this or you'd better not be doing this twenty years from now. And that was it. It was time to decamp before I went to the credit union and bought a car or got a loan for a house or something, and I'd be in hock to the company store. I believe that if I had stayed there one more year I would have been locked in. But when she asked me about that gift I realized that I was in a cycle. I knew this is what my parents were talking about.

Like many reentry women Marcie had a life event that reawakened a dormant dream. She knew that she had to return to college. She knew that she could earn a degree, but on her own terms. And so she faced what so many women face when they decide to go back to college. She faced people who had "told her so." People who had told her that college mattered, that she would regret her decision to drop out, and that one day she would have to return to complete her degree. Marcie had finally come to the conclusion that they were right and that with maturity and a new seriousness of purpose, she could make it this time.

So here I am. I quit my job and started my full-time pursuit of a degree. And when I say full-time pursuit, I mean full-time pursuit of a degree in a continuing education sort of way: find a job that has the flexibility of hours that is going to allow me to take at least one class so that I can continue towards the end of getting that degree. I might only take one class this semester but I might be able to take three the following semester. You just need the flexibility when you are doing continuing ed, and so I ended up first working retail because it was the most viable for me. And eventually I was managing a retail store. I was the one who was making the schedules so it's like—hey hey hey—I'll work every night, because I have classes in the morning or this semester I'm gonna work the 12–8 shift. For now I'm working an office job near the campus. I get up. I go to work. I report at 8:00 a.m. I leave in ten minutes so I can make my 9:00 a.m. class. At 8:59 a.m. the professor is greeting you. She lectures. She stops at 9:50. And then I leave campus and go back to work. My day ends around 6:00 p.m.

I've been on the continuing ed track for fucking ever. I started taking a class here, a class there—something fun so that you can get a good grade and you'll go to the class. Now I've started looking towards taking classes that you can apply towards your transcript. I need one more math class and a seminar to graduate. And I'm also working on two incompletes.

I had all these wonderful plans for coming back to the continuing education program and receiving my degree in political science and at the same time working on a minor in Education so I could get my certification. With a piece of paper in my hand, my personality, and the fact that I am trainable and viable and have a very logical mind, I can get a position that will set me nicely. I'm good at organizational skills. I have been lacking creature comforts for so long with this continuing ed thing. If I could just have a house that I could feel comfortable walking naked from my bedroom to the kitchen and back, I'd be happy. I'm tired of the Grand Debate: Ramen Noodles? Or are we going to splurge and have Campbell's Soup? It's very real and a part of my problem. Ideally, I would like to go to graduate school and maybe teach college here because I think I could have an impact. But I've been rethinking this 'cause you start thinking I'm thirty-four and it's taken me how long just to get here? I'd be a fifty-year-old college teacher with no tenure. I don't think I have the patience right now to even think about going to school anymore with no money.

Routinely, women who return to school after an absence of many years are surprised by how school and their new lives don't mesh—either economically or physically. Nontraditional women are faced with class schedules that are made to fit students who only have sleep habits to consider when choosing between an 8 a.m. class and a noon class. Marcie laments having to buy and learn to use a computer and reminisces about the good old days when typewriters were the order of the day.

One really hard thing is that my work schedule, which is designed to allow me to take classes, always conflicts with my instructor's office hours. You know I really can't go and talk to an instructor and I'm reduced to playing phone tag. It's a lot more difficult for people to understand what you're asking. You know they can't see the confusion. They can't see that you think you have it on your face when you don't have it. So that's why my mentors are my saving graces. I can see them when I can see them. I can go to their homes. I can stop by their offices anytime—even if I only get seven minutes.

And nobody told me that I needed a $3,000 machine to go to school. I don't have a computer. I don't have a word processor and assignments have to be on a word processor. I don't have it so it's a big hassle for me. I don't even type. And I'm like I can't do it. Word processing is my constant angst. So I get to school many times at 5:30 a.m. and 6:00 a.m. to borrow a computer.

One semester I sweated bullets. I needed to pay a back balance in order to register and then pay half of the projected balance. And I'm doing this. My parents are letting me stay in their home. I don't ask for any money from my Mom. But I'm trying to convince this financial aid official that what I can pay is sufficient and all he'll say to me is the same thing over and over—what he won't accept. And I'm asking, "But what can you accept?" This is my situation. This is my reality. It is not changing. I've come this far. I'm in school. I'm in the continuing education program." And he kept telling me what was needed. The "mutha" wouldn't give me no eye contact. I went through all these people and all these roadblocks to work out a way to get in school that quarter. I think if I had been an eighteen-year-old I wouldn't have been in school anymore. I would have taken what he said while he looked down at his paper and felt like I had been dismissed. But I refused to be dismissed! I can laugh about it now.

Ultimately, this is what separates reentry women from traditional college students—life experiences that help them laugh at the bizarre and discouragingly unfair. After so many ups and downs in her college life, Marcie says that a belief in God and a sense that life is supposed to be composed of ups and downs keeps her from giving up when things get bad. She feels that this wisdom has come with age.

There's humor in almost every situation. What you have to remember before you start laughing or crying or ranting or raving, reacting to whatever is going on around you is, "Is it worth all that?" And is it alright? Are you here? 'Cause my logic is, if I woke up, I'm supposed to be here today. Which means whatever comes I'm supposed to be able to handle in some type of way, 'cause otherwise, God would have clapped His hands and said, "Come on girlfriend. It's time." I'm not a holy roller, but I think you have to deal with the kind of environment that you find yourself in, which means you have to learn to bend. You know that rigidity will not allow you to survive. When you look at these right wing Christian people going out of their gourds because they made a mistake, it's because they are so busy looking for the perfect rule. If you don't bend with the situation that you find yourself in, you're gonna break. And I can't afford to break. 'Cause who am I? I'm a Black woman in America and that's as handicapped as you can get. And I can't remember what comedian said it but it's the truth. There's an automatic pilot that I think all Blacks have that deals with survival. Blacks are on survival mode at all times. But I can't say being a Black woman has equipped me to manage—just to survive. If I were a good manager I wouldn't be in this situation. I would have gotten this shit right the first time. And I'm trying to make a way out of no way. I don't have a pot to piss in or a window to throw it out of, but I want it. And this is how I have to go about getting it. I need the piece of paper.

So when I'm sitting there wondering if the financial aid man is gonna let me in school, because he does have the final say; and when I'm wondering if my name made the computer 'cause I didn't actually see her key it in, since I had to get back to work; and when my car is down and I take the train to school; and when I don't have money in my pocket to take the train back, I panic. But then I think, I woke up this morning and something's got to give. I woke up.

The Mentor, the Sisters, and the Boyfriend

According to Marcie and many other reentry women, some of the side benefits of returning to school are the discoveries that you make about yourself and about other people. Fortunately, Marcie discovered reserves of untapped personal strength that kept her going when she wanted to drop out of school again. Other extra blessings for Marcie were all of the mentors that she met along the way who understood her fight and decided for whatever reason to help her. Marcie also found that old relationships faded from the stress of a demanding new lifestyle.

There is this one professor who is my advisor and my emotional mentor. She is quick as a whip, a little person too. She always cuts to the crux of the matter. Since she is about seventy plus years of age, she has lived through Negress, Negro, Black, and African American. She actually went to one of the "Seven Sisters" (the elite all women's colleges in the northeastern U.S.). I was impressed with that fact. In her age group, to have been at that kind of institution is a rarity. She is as you leave her and the way she's gonna be when you find her again—constant. She has all these letters behind her name and she is quite published. She's sharp. She knows her stuff. I guess she has influenced me from the school standpoint but also in the way I look at people and interact with them. I'm drawn to her in part because she treats me like an adult and doesn't let me get caught up in the technicalities. She tells me well in advance when seminars and special projects are due because she knows that I'm doing a balancing act between school, work, and my other adult responsibilities.

And then I also receive support from other continuing ed students. There's a continuing ed association and we meet once a month. When I started dealing with them I was like, "I cannot come over here and sit and look at you people for two and a half hours." But the fellowship is good and it lets you know that your problems are really kind of piss poor, real pitiful. One woman is coming through a divorce. One woman has a new baby. One woman's mother just died. You also learn that other people have been where you are. So it works out. We'll share books. We bring covered dishes. We have a penny fund and we give little scholarships. It's nice.

Yet, my younger sister is my main support. You know with parents it's, "How did things go?" And the reply you give them is always the same, "Just fine." 'Cause if you really talk to them then things start spiraling and even when the problem is dead, done and over, they still go, "Yang, yang, yang." They don't know that I'm over there begging for an extra minute on the cash flow thing. It would upset them. But I can tell my younger sister. I can tell my girl all about it—how I was talking to the financial aid director and the "mutha" wouldn't even look at me. She's my support, my confidant.

But then not all relationships are supportive. I broke up with this guy. School did not affect the personal relationship, though he would say it did. It was so typical. I'd gone and picked up another English, adding to the transcript to take the place of those incompletes that have been there for five or nine years. He said, "You don't have time for me." He acted as if going to school was getting in the way. Like because I'm in school I'm thinking a different way. How could that be? We are doing the same things. We go to the car races. We go to the ball games. We sit and look at TV. We go to car races. We go to ball games. We work on cars together. We go to car races. It was not changing. I was spending the same amount of time with him. It was just male insecurity. And he is a graduate of an elite men's college. No time was not the problem! He just thought attention was being diverted from him.

It's a Different World

In remembering her first undergraduate days, Marcie recalls a school very different from the one she returned to some ten years later. Within these words you can find her fond memories, but you can also hear her many regrets. Marcie relates a past and a present that seem generations apart.

Going to a Black school was the smartest thing I ever did. But I lost my mind. I looked around and all of these other people were not going to class and you know I was making these road trips to visit other campuses. Friends are saying, "We're going down to this football game." And you're like getting in the car with them.

I went to class my first semester and part of my second semester. I had a great time. I visited damn near every Black campus in the southeastern region. At the time, we had fallen back into this Black is beautiful thing. Dark black skin will be included in the Black culture's ideal of beauty, not a fair skinned Black woman but a black Black woman. Whereas before I was kicked to the curve. You know, "No no no baby yo nose a spread a little too wide." Now I became popular because of my dark skin. It was weird because in high school I didn't get a date. And then I got to college and suddenly they switched up the rules. And the same type of people that didn't really speak to me are suddenly saying, "You are the most beautiful thing I have ever seen in my life. Will you go out with me?" You're a beautiful Black woman as opposed to a pecan brown woman as opposed to a paper bag brown woman as opposed to a sun kissed honey colored woman. And some of them are very genuine in their emotions, the radical brothers wearing their little caps and African medallions, but then you feel that when they take you home or to a function, it's show and tell like in elementary school. "Look mom, it's tall, it's dark, and it's articulate." It makes you feel uncomfortable. I had a problem with that, but I ended up having a great time in college anyway.

After bouncing around to several colleges, Marcie feels that she has found her place. She attended a Black women's college. Although she admits that her choice of school was happenstance, she is quick to delineate the benefits of this setting. She finds the atmosphere comfortable and many of the professors, particularly the Black women, nurturing.

There are students who are able to be heard that would never be heard in a classroom at a White large state university. I've been in those large predominately White settings and I know they'd never be heard. You are heard because you are in a Black women's school and the Black woman instructor will look up and ask if they have something to say. She will take time to draw that student out in class. Whereas in another place that little flicker of a question in her eyes wouldn't have been noticed. There are things that are known by association that would never be known on a larger campus. You run into the same instructors. The professors, because they are Black women, also remember what it's like not to be heard in class. Any silencing in this setting would be more messy—class issues. You know we have our own, "I'm light, I'm bright, I'm darn near White, and you're dark and you don't have hair" issues. There are some contradictions. For instance, all of that reach out and help somebody—reach back into the community—only applies so long as the community is not next door. There are definite class issues among the Black elite, who also want to be as far from the ghetto as their White peers.

Marcie's first experience with college was not successful. She lists several possible reasons that are often heard in the stories of other reentry women: she was young and immature or it was not the right kind of institution. Now Marcie has returned to college, older and wiser. She's also attending a Black women's college that she attended earlier. In spite of all the commonalities between Mar-

cie, the professors, and the young Black women students, Marcie still feels that
being older makes her different.

It would be lovely to say that I went to a Black women's college for some
high minded reason—you know the warmth of my sisterhood. I'm at this
Black women's college because I had been here before and they were pleased
enough with my work to remember it. So it was the easiest place to gain entry.
I'll be honest. I had tried a state school. I had always heard it was a dummy
school. I couldn't get in that place if I had to, not with my GPA because they
were not willing to take the chance. They were going with just the facts
ma'am—just the facts. And the facts on paper were that I'm not a viable student. And I'm not here to prove those facts wrong. I'm here to get a piece of
paper. I'm not going to graduate with a 3.0 I'm not going to graduate cum
laude, just Oh, Lordie.

Yet it's true that in a classroom setting because you have so many Black
women—I'm gonna say Black girls, some of these kids could technically have
been my children—it's different. There is a sense of empowerment but I don't
believe it's reality based at all. And that is because I've been out in the real
world already. And you hear these girls say things like, "In my opinion."
They're so emphatic. Naivete! I think everybody goes through this. They are
young and trying so desperately to be adult. I know this isn't the real world.
When I was here before, the students were reality based. Our hands were a lot
more in the community. We were coming off of the 1970s Black power thing.
Sitting and listening to these girls, they're frightened of the surrounding community. They've been cushioned and pulled away. The difference is societal.

These girls don't see clearly. They only interact with the children who
went to the same elementary schools and who were involved in the same social clubs, Jack and Jill, and dit, dit, dit. They were probably in the same debu-
tante class. They probably know each other from the National Medical Association or the National Dental Association. So they don't know how to speak
to old lady Johnson.

The stratification is a lot more vast now. You had the monied Blacks, the
doctor, lawyer, school teacher, and ah preacher's children back in the '50s and
early '60s going to school. But then you had people like my mom, she was on
the five-year plan, which meant that you work one semester and go to school
the next semester. When I was here before there was a middle, middle class of
students. Now you have kids that are either rolling in money, money, money or,
those who are in a crunch for tampons.

Marcie marvels at how the changes in society have brought about changes
at her former institution. The new sexual revolution as it is expressed on campus
is unsettling. She thinks that the traditional college woman student thinks and
depends too much on men.

They talk about, "my man." I'm thinking, "Your man? What do you mean your man?" My man includes the years that it takes to get that relationship on track. My man says you have actually administered medications when he was sick. We never made references like that. It was like, boyfriend or I'm seeing this guy. There's this facade or image thing that's big with this generation. He drives a BMW. He is wearing Armani. He bought me Halston, or Lauren or whatever the cologne is at the moment. They think that because it drives a BMW and its daddy is rich he won't kick your ass. They think this. They think that the way he talks down to you is just his nervousness. They are abused girls. We did have guys that were beating on the girls, but this thing is crazy right now. The girls are so desperate for attention, so desperate to feel loved by someone.

You have a set of girls that change clothes at least three times a day. And they all have hair weaves. Do you know how much money is spent on hair weaves? If you're bald, you're bald. But they want it like Whoopi says, cas-ca-scading. Hair is really not that important. But they like have this facade. They think if my hair is like this famous movie star then I'm that character. It's frightening for me to see. It's all for show, impressing the guys. They don't see the guys as necessary bread the way my mother or even my generation saw them, as a meal ticket. They see them as necessary in an emotional, social sense, validation.

There was one girl on the phone outside one of the exit doors begging and pleading with this guy. When she got off the phone she was sniffling. So I called my taxi and sat there. And I said, "I'm not going to ignore the fact that you're crying. Whatever it is I know it hurt but you need to know this. I know it sounds like I'm trivializing how you're feeling right now, but if you plan on making it out of college without being slain, with all the emotional contretemps that you're gonna run into, I'm gonna give you some advice. There is a 3-F rule. It's a very hard rule and it can be modified depending on the situation you're in. If this person is not feeding you, fucking you and financing you, then they are of absolutely no importance in the scheme of things. Period! And feeding and finance are big on the list. If he can help you get out of school then you cry for him. But if he can't, you need to figure out what needs to be done in time for your next class and deal with him when you're off the clock.

Returning to a school that you previously attended can be difficult because invariably things will have changed. Yet, many reentry women go back to schools that they once dropped out of in order to reclaim credits or in search of something familiar and safe. These reasons certainly prompted Marcie's return.

The youngest of the eight women who have shared their stories about going to school as nontraditional students, Marcie is typically reflective about missed opportunities and is ever aware of how her college educated siblings and friends lead different and more privileged lives because of their educations. Being in the middle of the upper middle class lives of her parents and friends, Marcie is painfully aware of why she must earn her degree—in order to make more money, have better jobs, and live up to her parents' and her own hopes. She seems to lead a life shadowed by these expectations.

CHAPTER 4

Jean:
Planting New Flowers

"And I have this new life. What do I do? It's either go to school or plant flowers in the yard." Jean's life changed forever with her husband's sudden death. After thirty-one years of marriage they were settling into their empty nest and both succeeding in their careers. Jean chaired the school's physical education program while her husband served as an assistant principal at one of the city's premier high schools. One weekend Jean's husband died of an asthma-induced heart attack while he was at the post office mailing letters. She explained that her world had a hole in it. The filler became school. Millions of nontraditional women return to college because there is now room in their lives. This second reentry experience helped her with a difficult transition, providing structure and purpose. During one of our many visits we worked together in her front yard planting azalea bushes. She said that she knew she would be alone the rest of her life and that going to school and planting flowers would be enough for her. I joked with her about being too young and too full of life to just go to school and plant flowers. She maintained that her life's course was set.

Introduction

Jean is an energetic woman in her early fifties. She has a booming contralto voice that seems too big for her small-boned body. She speaks deliberately, peering occasionally over her large glasses to make sure that she is being understood. The director of her middle school's physical education program, her quick movements are indicative of her high energy level and the fitness that her chosen discipline demands. Jean has a skin coloring that resembles a walnut shell's pale creamy beige. Her face is devoid of lines except for those that were etched about her eyes by her frequent smiles. She often sits in a yoga position with one leg folded neatly over the other and occasionally squats in the chair with her chin resting on her knee.

A first generation college student, she was born in a small southern town to a middle class family. Her father was the local mortician and the president of the local Black school board and her mother was a housewife. She was one of five children, two girls and three boys and ranked at "the bottom of the bowl" as the youngest. Her family emphasized education. Four of the five children have college educations. After a traditional undergraduate program, Jean reentered school on three occasions, completing master's and specialist's degree programs.

I'm certified in K-12. I've gone back to school three times. Presently I'm working on my middle grades certificate. I teach health and physical education. Before this school enrollment, I completed certification for social studies for the secondary level, which was an upgrade of my undergraduate degree.

I don't know whether I want a change of career or not. I'm still in an indecisive stage. I'm trying to decide exactly whether I want to make the change for secondary or stay in the middle grades. My six-year degree will probably be in middle grades.

Like countless women who returned to school after their thirties, Jean's reentry was connected to employment. Not only do they, as did Jean, work toward a degree so that they can progress in their jobs, but frequently they are attempting to sort out their careers, change career directions, or acquaint themselves with other career options.

Part of the reason that I returned to school was for the cost of living raise that school teachers get from the board of education for upgrading their level of certification. It's a substantial increase in pay. However, the main reason that I returned to school was because most of my coworkers were returning to school not only to get their degrees but in an attempt to venture into administration. In the immediate area where I work there are four of us in the gym. So I figured that as the chairman of the department and the one who makes the decisions my educational level should not be lower than that of my employees, especially since they are younger. I thought I had better upgrade my educational level.

In returning to school, I found that I stood out like a sore thumb because I was a bit antiquated. When I looked around the classroom there were all these young energetic minds. However, I felt that I had a lot to give because of the experience that I brought to the classroom. I had lived longer than they had, and I had so many years as a teacher in the classroom. Many of these young people were getting ready to go into the classroom for the first time as teachers. Things would come up in class that you couldn't find answers to in the book. I was able to adjust to that and to have answers because I probably had been there or knew someone who had.

The students were so young and very philosophical. Maybe they picked it up in their readings or maybe from their travels, but they talked in terms of what the world should be and of what they would like to see. Their opinions weren't based on experience like mine, but on what they dreamed. That was refreshing. I was able to learn from them and they were able to learn from me.

God Bless the Child That's Got Her Own

One idea that is constantly repeated by mature women who are entering or reentering higher education is that they are different from their younger counterparts because their understanding of the world is more informed. They utter phrases like, "I know the game," or "It's not personal. It's just the way things go." With this awareness and sense of purpose, reentry women carry with them a real urgency, a determined sense of purpose, and the knowledge that it will not be easy or fair.

There have been times when I knew that I was not being dealt with fairly by instructors. On one particular occasion, during an exam, one of the students asked if she could go to a nearby coffee shop and do her exam. The professor gave her permission. The next time I asked if I could do the same thing and was met with a point blank, "No." He said that his previous behavior was to prove a point, that he trusted his students. I asked him to prove another point. The answer remained, "No." I can't say what the truth of this situation was, but I have my suspicions. This classroom dilemma was pretty uncomfortable for me. But I've learned by now that things are not always fair. I just dealt with my feelings and so did the rest of the class. They were all looking on.

I understand that it's difficult to manage a classroom. I've been there. When I'm the teacher I try to deal fairly with all people and not to show differences. I try to make examples that won't make anyone feel uncomfortable. I try to have an open environment so that if someone needs to talk they will be confident in coming forward with whatever they have on their minds. That way we can all get answers and share. You never know what might benefit someone else and might help to get a point across. I stand back and roll with the punches. I don't feel a need to be in charge. When something unpleasant happens in my classroom or when I'm in the other role as student, I try to remember that I am an adult. I don't get upset.

Another difficult moment occurred in a state history class when we had to deal with the Civil Rights Movement and the overt prejudices that existed between Blacks and Whites in our area. There were a lot of historic events that occurred in our state. I was the only Black in the class and to add to that I was the oldest student which meant that I had the opportunity not only to read of the changes but I had lived through the changes we were discussing. There were times in this class when my presence made the professor uncomfortable. There were times, I'm sure, when even he would have liked to or needed to ask me questions.

Everyone was uncomfortable because there would be lots of twisting, turning, squirming, fidgeting. Movements that let me know that the classroom atmosphere was not what it seemed. The teacher would not be able to look at me at these times. He'd bat his eyes, look away, or try to change the tone or direction of the conversation. To be honest, after a while, I felt that it was better for everyone if I limited my remarks. So there were questions that I did not respond to and others that I didn't respond to sincerely. I suppressed my own answers to questions and reactions to comments.

Probably the most uncomfortable moment that I ever had in school came during my master's program. It was shortly after the school systems were integrated. The professor stood up and asked, "How did you feel when you first walked into a classroom and you had to teach children of a different race?" The classroom was quiet. And I happened to have a watch. I watched as the second hand on my watch went around. One woman cleared her throat. I raised my hand and said, "What do you mean when all of a sudden you are teaching children of a different race? We have been teaching children of a different race all of our lives even though we were the ones with the limited education. We taught them what the bathroom was for and what to do when they went in there and what the spoon and fork was for and where to place them after they picked them up off the table. We even chewed up their food and put it in their mouths. There were times when we even breast fed them, even though some of them don't want to admit it now. So we did not all of a sudden start teaching children of a different race. We taught them all the time. But once they got up large enough to open their mouths and say that "word" we had to start saying "Yes ma'am" and "Yes sir" to them. There was silence again in that room, a longer silence.

That was one of those times when I should have been quiet. It would have been better if I had not made that particular statement. I upset some feelings. And I needed the grade for this class. I knew that school wasn't the fair place it's cracked up to be and that when pencil marking time came the teacher would have the last word. But I couldn't help myself that time. I could tell by the teacher's reaction that I had gone too far. I had also forgotten that I was there for a purpose and that was to acquire the knowledge and to get a decent grade out of the course. But I had to make the decision then and there on the spot and I did. I could not let the teacher fail to recognize the history of the women folk who came before me. I was also old enough to remember. I was old enough to know better.

We want to believe that things have gotten better between Blacks and

Whites but deep down we know that they have really not. Integration has sugar coated some aspects. However, I do feel that in my lifetime I have formed some relationships with Whites that are genuine. But these relationships were formed typically because we were thrown together and had to survive together. Had it not been for the circumstances of being forced together the relationships would not have existed.

I wish it were that when you get to this level of education the challenge is all in the individual learning. Of course there is exertion. You must expect to put forth a real effort at this level, as you climb. You'll be exposed to more. You'll grow overall as a person, but it is not all fair. I wish that it were that way with school. Yet I find that school is just like the rest of life. However, it has been a real opportunity. It has made me stretch. I've had lots of help along the way. When I've had problems I have not had any problems seeking and finding help. And I go where it presents itself. I don't limit or reject a helping hand just 'cause it comes from a particular race.

Jean, believing that school is a mirror of the circumstances she often faces in life, sees her reentry process as a series of negotiations. Like many other reentry women, she makes arrangements with classmates, family members, and friends, in attempts to meet her obligations. According to Jean, it can be difficult to negotiate her predominately White school setting because not everyone is accepting or friendly, but she feels that she has also learned how to cope with this environment.

There's a little circle that you find yourself being able to be a part of if you have the ability to get along with people as I do. I find that I am more or less a people person. I do know that there are some White students who will have little or no interactions with me after class. Yet some of the other students will get together with me to study. Some of that stems over into lasting relationships. When our paths cross outside of the class there are students who will stop and hold conversations with me and invite me out. Whereas some of the students I've gone to school with refuse to acknowledge me outside of class. I've learned to get my lead from the other person. If I don't get an indication that they are willing to deal with me then I don't make a step. I lived through integration. I've adjusted to the new rules. I'm not uncomfortable with this because I'm from the old school. It's still all about power, who has it and who lacks it.

Jean does not acknowledge whether or not it bothers her to know that classroom liaisons are tenuous and context dependent. She chalks up the teeter-totter nature of such alliances to society's unwritten and unexpressed understanding between Blacks and Whites in America. In addition, she covers her feelings regarding this impasse by explaining that as a Black woman, she can tolerate the ambiguity.

I feel that the Black woman is strong. I don't mean to belittle any other race or to say that other women are not equally strong. But because of our trials and tribulations we (Black women) have had to work twice as hard, to endure tremendous pain, just to survive. Endurance and the need to survive, to cope with situations throughout the ages has made us strong. Now that works for us and also against us. We have to work so hard and it is not always known. Others think that they work hard but ways are made and doors are opened for people who think that they do it for themselves. We (Black women) have to push to get that door open. It's not always what you know in school. It is often who you know. Most of the professors behind the desks and the people of power behind all the glass doors in the world are White. Perhaps they didn't have to struggle as hard. Who knows? Perhaps they are there because of who they knew or who their families knew. It's like the words to that Billie Holiday tune, "Them that's got shall get. Them that's not shall lose . . . But God bless the child that's got his own." I just feel that there is a difference made in the school setting between Black students and others. But then that's just life. I don't like to think that way. That's the way that it is. It is challenging.

Educated in Romance

So many of the choices made by reentry women—marriage, children, and career choices—were made when they were younger and "naive." They make statements like, "I thought I was supposed to get married," or "Those were the choices that women had then." These assertions suggest that many of their earlier decisions were influenced by family and societal expectations. As Jean indicates, love and the choices of starting a family swayed her life options. However, there are few indications that such decisions controlled or affected the school or career paths of the men in their lives.

Neither of my parents actually finished school in terms of going to a building, a formal program, and graduating. Both were self-educated and my father went to trade school to learn brick masonry. He worked in that area for years until his health no longer allowed it. Then he went back to trade school and trained as a mortician. My mother's formal education ended in the eighth grade. At the time though that was considered really good. I'm the youngest in the family. The bottom of the bowl. We all went to college. But one of my brothers decided that college was not for him.

At one time, I wanted to go into the service. It seemed like it would be an exciting life. But my brothers, who had been in the military, turned me around. So most of my guidance and support came from my family. In my undergraduate days I was so busy falling in love that I had to fight to maintain a decent grade point average. When I was on my way to college, I met my husband on the train. That stands out as my most pleasant school experience ever. It had already been an exciting day for me. I had been competing in a statewide rhetorical contest as the winner from my district. Several hours later I was on board a train and was on my way to school. At that time I didn't know that I would marry him, but I knew that it was a special meeting.

This is not the first time that I've gone back to school to pursue my master's. I decided at another time that I wanted to pursue my master's. But I had to commute to and from college and the traveling after school got to be a little more than I could handle. The fact that I was having and raising young children greatly contributed to the decision to quit school. I just couldn't hold up to the demands. So it would be fifteen or twenty years before I went back to school. I was out of school for quite while.

I Can Take Anything for a Year or Two

Jean saw school as a major change in her life. Her first reentry was cut short by her realization that her family life was too demanding to fit in a master's program. She prepared mentally for her subsequent two reentry school experiences by delving in with the knowledge that "it won't be forever." Each school journey, to her master's and specialist's degrees, were approached with the end ever in mind, if not necessarily in sight, and was done on a part-time basis. She did them, taking one course each quarter and doubling up in the summer months when she was on leave from teaching.

My work day ends at 3:45 and class usually starts at 4 o'clock. I work only a couple of minutes from the college campus so I grab a sandwich, eat it in the parking lot, and rush to class. I always feel my brain functions better if my stomach is happy. The down time in the car helps me come down from the day's frustrations and helps me gear up for the next venture. Besides it helps me go to class with a better attitude. After all I was not pressured to be back in school. It was something that I wanted to do and I always kept that in mind. It was a good experience. I got a chance to meet a lot of people who were also trying to better themselves.

Classes usually ended about 8:30 or 9 o'clock. Usually I picked something up on my way home or my husband would have prepared a snack for me. We'd sit around and talk. We both needed that. He had his master's already. He would actually help. When I needed a certain book he would sometimes scout around for it. When I told him that I absolutely had to have a computer he checked his computer out of work and let me use it. He also supported me in other ways, extra gas and lunch money. He was my backbone, my supporter, my best friend. When I had a test coming up, he would drill me on the materials. What can I say? He was my confidant.

I never touched assignments after class because my day had already been too long. My class days were never back to back and this gave me a chance to prepare. I usually did my studying when the house was quiet. After I finished supper the next day, I'd focus on studying, either going to the library or finding another place that was still—no television, music, or distractions. I tried to budget my time so that I wouldn't get behind in my studies. But things did have a way of overlapping: housework, family chores, and just dealing with family problems. And then there are the outside obligations: church activities, social organizations, clubs, and community work. I stopped accepting offices in my clubs because I couldn't give both school and them 100 percent.

Luckily, I was the type of person that liked to study late at night or early in the morning. I would go to bed with my husband at 11 o'clock, set the alarm for 3:00 or 4:00 a.m., then get up and do my studying. That way I could still have our family time and my study time too. In terms of my relationship with my husband, he had to step up his family responsibilities, preparing more meals. He did his part, especially when I had to study. When I was in class, of course he was left to get his own meals and to eat them alone. I think it could have affected us had we not had our priorities in order. We both knew that it was not something that would not go on forever. It was only for a short time. You give it what it takes to accomplish your goal. I can endure anything for a year or two.

Like many women who are married and return to school, the house and its accompanying chores continue to be their responsibility. When a husband attempts to share some of the burden he is acknowledged as a supportive hero. Stories from returning college women show that the proportion of work assumed by supportive spouses does not correspond to what is actually needed. Consequently, the married women who return to school still perform most of the household chores while attending school. However, when male spouses return to school, they are usually released from any duty which interferes with school. In addition, many wives, like Jean, find inventive ways to keep school from interrupting their normal lives.

Jean finished her master's and specialist's degrees. Her joy for living returned. She recently retired from teaching and is always busy working in the community and traveling. And although she continues to plant flowers she does not plant them alone. She has remarried and lives in a new house with many new flowers.

CHAPTER 5

Beth:
I Was Never Good Enough

Beth's early schooling experiences of being excluded because she was poor set the tone for elementary, middle school, high school, and inevitably her college reentry years. Her narrative weaves concerns about fitting in with thoughts about being regarded as inferior. Twenty years later, she still remembers the trauma of a school environment where she was teased relentlessly for wearing "homemade clothes" and for having only biscuits and syrup for lunch. Trying to fit and to be "just as good" resonates throughout many reentry women's stories and Beth's words ring with the familiarity of an outsider who desperately wants to gain admission.

Introduction

A petite woman with a hesitant girlish manner, Beth is the birth mother of three children and stepmother to three others. Her youngest child is fifteen and her oldest is twenty. A career military wife, she has traveled extensively for the last eighteen years with her second husband. The fifth of six children and a first-generation college student, Beth grew up poor in the rural South. She attends a religious-affiliated women's college and feels empowered by the small classroom setting.

Beth's overcompensation for a life begun in poverty is aptly reflected in her conservative blue-suited business attire, in her deliberate enunciation of each word, and in too-perfect erect posture. Her thin, angular face features narrow, intense black eyes, yet the initial hesitancy of her glances betray the forcefulness of her personality. She jokingly describes herself as a woman driven to finally get her college degree.

The way teachers treated me in the early years shaped my attitude towards school. I wouldn't say that my grades were bad, it was just that they could have been much better. It seemed like I was wasting my time in school. No teacher ever took time with me.

Also I never had any interest in school because I did a lot of hard work as a child. I came from a single-parent home. My father passed when I was two years old. My mother raised six children (five girls and one boy) by working two jobs. She was basically gone most of the time just trying to provide. It was our responsibility to take care of home. We really didn't have time to get into extracurricular activities. It was church and running errands for various folks in the neighborhood. I took care of elderly people in my neighborhood. So I didn't stay after school to do things like most kids. I didn't have the time.

Beth continues to view the world through this veil of deprivation. Ever conscious of her material surroundings, she speaks occasionally of how it comforts her that she is attending an exclusive school with an elegant setting, historic architecture, and substantial art holdings. Her present upper-middle class background consoles this adult who speaks with a child's voice of the pain of hunger and wanting so much more than she had.

I didn't have very many clothes when I was coming up. Once my sister, who was much older and used to sew for the family, bought some beautiful fabric and promised to make me a skirt. But I couldn't wait for her to sew it, so I took the material, wrapped it around me, and went to school. Certainly the day I wore that skirt turned out to be very humiliating because the popular girls discovered that it wasn't a real wrap skirt and teased me about it for about a week.

After daddy died our family had a hard time. It was embarrassing for me that we were so poor that I couldn't buy my lunch like most of my friends. I had to take biscuits with syrup on them. I wanted a hot school lunch like everybody else. I know I shouldn't complain because some people didn't have lunch. But it wasn't all bad. While I may not have had the clothes that I wanted to wear, mama was fortunate to work in White folks' homes. They gave us a lot of things and so our house was more comfortable than most because of the things that we had, hand-me-down clothes and furniture. A lot of our friends thought we had it going on. In some ways, we were living better than some of our teachers. Our house stayed spotless because my mother was a strong ruler and she had five girls taking care of things. Mama believed that you had to appreciate and learn to take care of what you had.

Despite the hard work, I had quite a pleasant childhood. What I did away from school was fun. Considering there were so many girls in the family there were always plenty of people hanging around. Our girlfriends would visit and that made boys gravitate towards our house. We had a lot going on for children who were restricted to the house while their mother worked.

In general, I guess, well, the elementary years were not that pleasant because teachers didn't give people from single-parent homes that much attention. If your parents didn't attend PTA meetings and participate in the school social scene, they (the teachers) felt that your family had no interest in your schooling and so they didn't care either. In addition, they didn't spend that much time with you if you came from a lower socio-economic background. They had their favorites and their picks. Even though my teachers were Black, there was a class system going on back then that was based on color. The ones that had less or weren't bright enough just didn't get it. Being light skinned and having "good" hair is what they called "cutting the cake." It's those differences right within our own culture that hurt me.

I was a dark-skinned, nappy-haired child and I was viewed unfavorably. Since I had all three things (poverty, a single-parent household, and a dark complexion) working against me, they didn't give me the time of day. My teachers didn't make school very interesting for me and, therefore, I didn't make it interesting for myself.

I went to an all-Black school until my eighth-grade year and then I went to an integrated high school. Going to an integrated school was better because things were beginning to change in the sixties. While I recognized my new White classmates for being different, I basically did what I had to do and went on my way. It wasn't a dilemma for me seeing all that they had and wanting to have what they had. I couldn't keep up with my own people (Blacks), so I knew I couldn't keep up with White people. So integration didn't impact me that much. My surroundings didn't change. I was bussed over there and bussed out. Mostly Whites were just as afraid of us as we were of them. There were not outbreaks in our school.

The White teachers weren't so class conscious as far as what you could do and what you couldn't do. I learned a little more after the schools were integrated. It was probably because the new teachers thought all Black students were deficient. They didn't know about our bright-skinned and curly hair biases. This had no significance for my new White teachers. I found it easier to talk to them. Yet my family situation still made somewhat of a difference because my mother couldn't attend functions like parent-teacher conferences.

By the time I got to high school my grades had already started falling. And no one was going to reach back that far to pick me up. And then it didn't help my chances in high school that I could never participate in extracurricular activities. There was no way for me to get attention through any type of sports or group activities.

But I had it better than a lot of people because I had the kind of mother who talked to you and taught you about life. One thing that she would say to us was, "Unfair things are going to happen to you because you are poor. That's society. But it doesn't have to control what you are or what you become." Those are the facts of life you learn when you have only one parent. My mother was aware of this because of the jobs she was forced to hold. She'd grit her teeth and do what she had to do. She was very proud and knew that working menial jobs did not make you menial. You do what you have to do to survive and you keep your mouth shut.

By my senior year in high school I began to make better grades for some odd reason which I cannot explain. This time is my most pleasant memory of school. I was able to do more, go on dates, and participate in activities. Yet I never anticipated life getting so serious so soon. It was a sad feeling seeing my youth come to an end. I was separating from my friends. Many of them were going to college. I was getting married. I didn't have any plans for college. I just wanted to get out of high school. Everybody else had plans for going to college. That was the last thing on my mind because of my socialization.

Things would have probably been much different in my life had I had a father. I finished high school on May 8 and got married on May 16. I think I married so young because I was looking for a husband, someone to take care of me.

My new husband went into the military. He was busy, going to work every-day, doing things that were important, and I was just a housewife. We started our family immediately and had three children. I would see women joining the military and making something of themselves and there I was stuck with three kids with no outlet. We stayed married seven years. Even from the onset of the marriage, I knew that it would never last. After the divorce I had to work. I would get jobs in cafeterias, mess halls, cleaning up school buildings, and things like that.

Beth felt insecure and hopeless in her new life of raising children alone and working jobs for little pay with no future. She saw school as a way out and looked around for a program that would quickly give her marketable skills. While training at a vocational technical college, Beth met and married her second husband. He had three children and Beth had three children. Their home became a "Brady Bunch" situation. She feels that her attraction to him was based in part on his desire to have more—a good education and a better future.

When I got the opportunity to go to school I decided to take up secretarial science. At first I couldn't get admitted into the program because my high school grade point average was too low. I had always felt inadequate and this made me feel worse. I was retested and retested until I finally got accepted into the program. The test was very intimidating. But I went for it. I graduated and it was the most thrilling thing that I had ever experienced aside from graduating from high school. It was victorious just marching across the stage.

I worked as a secretary for five years. Occasionally I took brown bag courses and night classes at area institutions. The night courses were usually to keep me busy or to help me with a job.

This testing of the waters is a common phenomenon among reentry women. Many women, in an attempt to judge whether or not they can handle school, participate in non-degree courses in their communities. Such ventures aid them in determining if they have the ability to learn new information and if they will be able to add new responsibilities to their lives.

Past Regrets

I've always wanted to have a degree. I think in those former school years I wasted so much time. I guess those old memories are baggage that I'm still carrying around. It's just hard to put that stuff down. A lot of people say, "Hey just get over it." Some things just stay with you forever. I mean just thinking about it, the color structure that I grew up with, brings back the pain of being a child. It's sad what we did to ourselves. The teachers in school who were supposed to be role models didn't care for us. I hear my husband and his friends talk about how their teachers stayed on their backs and made them work. That's how it should have been for me. I came from an entirely different world. He talks about the grief he took from his English teacher, Mrs. Woodard. It grieves me just to hear him talk about it. I wish I had someone to mentor me with that kind of spirit. I caught hell. I was always brushed aside.

I just thank God that my children have totally different backgrounds than I had. They were reared to be "A" students. I was reared to make "C's" and "D's." It was hard sitting in class and being ill-equipped to handle the work. My mother only had a tenth-grade education so she couldn't help me with schoolwork. Teachers wouldn't take the time to show me anything. They'd put it on the board. Zoom. Zap. It was gone. It was the most humiliating thing just sitting there in the classroom and not knowing what was going on.

I recall it was the hardest thing trying to learn my times tables because I was not good at memorizing things. Now I know that there is a pattern to it. But no one told me this when I needed to know it. I cringed whenever I was called on to do a math problem. I also hated reading. Luckily, I was usually skipped over because the teacher catered to a select few. If the teacher felt that you couldn't do it she wouldn't call on you. It was the same thing with parts for school plays and other activities. They (the teachers) had their favorites. They didn't pick kids like me so that we wouldn't embarrass ourselves or our school. Good thing I couldn't participate anyway. I always had to go straight home after school.

Even though the pain is still there I know that the pain is what made me the way I am today. Those negative experiences molded me. When I look at my children, I feel so good to see them take a lead in school. They are so energetic. They are getting a chance to do things that I didn't get a chance to do. And they don't take a back seat whether the teacher acknowledges them or not. It makes all the difference in the world to me. I have to say thank God that they don't have to do what I had to do.

It has been a long road for Beth, the one from technical school to a prestigious women's college. And it was partly determination with a good mix of fortunate timing that led her to "all of this."

My second husband's job meant relocating. When we moved here the district superintendent of our religious denomination came to welcome us and asked if I planned to get a job. I responded rather casually that I would like to go to school. He told me that our denomination had a women's college nearby and that there were funds available to help me. I said that it had to be more complicated than that and he said, "No. Just call Ms. Johnson and go on over." I went over the next day and Ms. Johnson took me to the campus.

Getting the letter of acceptance to this college was the most pleasant thing that ever happened. I mean I had never dreamed that I would be accepted into an institution like this. It's mainly White and a women's college. I'm not cut from this fabric. I had never considered the thought. I've always wanted to go back to college but I never thought it would be in such a grand setting.

When I was growing up, college wasn't talked about in my household. Deep down inside I knew that I could do it, especially after seeing others in my peer group succeed. Although I want to do this mainly for me, I also want my children to have confidence so that they can aspire to higher goals. I want to, by example, make them want to go to college. I know that when I hear the younger White students in my class talk, they don't know anything else. College was just the next step. It was something that was expected, "I need to go to college so that I can . . . " In my house it was, "You need to get a husband. You need to get a job."

I feel victorious about being here at this school. I feel that I am achieving something that my forefathers worked so hard for. And I'm getting the opportunity they earned. Furthermore, I'm getting to do this while my kids are around. I can inspire them to do things. It's just a personal thing for me.

I'm Not Your Typical Student

I get up around 4:30 and 5:00 in the morning and meditate. Then if it is a class day I review before school. I get the kids up around 5. The kids at home are 16 and 17. They usually do their own breakfast and fix mine also.

I usually leave home about 8:30 once the kids are gone. I go to the library 'cause my classes don't start until 9:45. I'm in school Monday through Friday. Basically I'm there until 3:30 or 4:00 p.m. everyday. Then I pick up the kids from school.

It's a lot of studying once I get home. The majority of my time is spent reading and yet it seems like sometimes I don't get any further. My husband thinks that I work too hard and that I'm not always learning efficiently because I'm too serious. He feels that I need to relax. But it's almost impossible for me to relax. I feel like I'd be wasting my time. And I've already wasted too much time. My husband has to remind me when I've been at it too long. He has had to lay down the law and make me go to bed at 10 o'clock. We've agreed on this.

When I returned to school I felt that I was lacking as a student. A good example of this is the physics class that I was required to take. I tried so hard. I wanted to know and understand the material. I was lost. The majority of the younger students had physics, biology, chemistry, and calculus in high school. I had not had these subjects. It was a new ball game for me. I was forever asking questions. A couple of students have told me that I was too aggressive. I was just voicing my opinions. But I've noticed that most of the older students don't say much in class. Later they (the older students) will talk privately. They'll ask me questions after class instead of asking them of the teacher during class. I feel like I shouldn't have to walk away from the classroom not understanding what I'm paying for. I sometimes just take it upon myself to hold the professor responsible for my learning. Sometimes I scuffle with the material because I'm not familiar with the terminology. I'll explain to the professors that I don't have an adequate background or the same background as others and ask for extra help. I don't feel that I'm aggressive.

If there is something that I need and I know another student has the answer or resources, I ask. For the most part they (the younger students, Whites) have been helpful. Only once when I asked a student to explain something did I get a cold shoulder. The student I approached told me to ask the teacher. I didn't let that bother me. You have to rise above your circumstances. You are going to get a snobby one every now and then.

I'm here for an education. The small classroom setting is good for me. I know my purpose. They would have to lock the doors to keep me out. I'm breaking ground for my sisters (Black women) and for the children who will come after me. I see the subtleties. A lot of the students in my classes had mothers and grandmothers that were in school here. They know the terrible reputation that this school had concerning Blacks. I've heard negative things about the history of this school and Blacks. A lot of the books in the archives about the history of the school are sealed and that is suspicious. And some of that sentiment is alive and well and kicking in this very environment. They know the whole deal, even things I don't know. Whether the rumors about the school's involvement with the Klan are true or not, I don't know.

I see that there is a high turnover rate on campus for Black students, but living off campus you don't get the full effect. I'm sure that being a Black person and an older student, and considering that these girls are between seventeen and twenty, affects how they deal with me. These girls are probably a little careful about what they would say to an older person versus what they might say to a younger Black person. Most of the young Black students who stay on campus stay just one semester.

All of the controversy aside, Beth feels that her focus must remain on her schoolwork. She continues to see herself as the student she was in earlier years who just didn't understand even when concepts were written on the board. Her first semester in school was particularly difficult. She recalled having a history teacher who only gave comprehensive essay tests. Beth's phobia of trying to memorize information like times tables and reproduce it made her so anxious that she considered quitting school.

I'm concerned that I'm not a good writer. I have always been intimidated by writing. I'll read something someone else has written and say, "Oh my goodness. Look at these mistakes." But I can't do that with my work. Probably a crisis point came for me in my very first semester. I had a history professor who only gave essay tests. I could not sit there and write two essays after we had talked about this subject for an entire week. I was devastated that the professor expected us to do this. I was frightened. She told me to calm down. She acted like it was no big deal. It was just the fact that you have to sit there and write two essays, one long and one short. It was going to be 60 percent of the course grade. I had all of this stuff in my head. We had studied so much, at least fifteen different things, and I would have to write on two things. I actually studied but when it came time for the test, I knew nothing. I could not regurgitate any of it. I couldn't put what I knew on that piece of paper.

I was so afraid of failure that I couldn't even finish the test. Everything just went out of my head. I was so intimidated by the test. I failed. But the professor encouraged me to take it again. She went over the first exam with me and pointed out exactly what I had done wrong. I needed the coaching and the reinforcement. She knew that I needed the encouragement. She didn't fall for what I was showing on the outside. She didn't think that I was as strong as I pretended to be. And I wasn't. She gave me another chance. I'll never forget that because not too many people have ever given me a second chance.

In my class I'm looking at girls from seventeen through twenty. Many times there is only one other older student. And I'll generally know when she's (the older student) struggling because we will confide in each other. But the younger set seems to know what's going on most of the time. The younger women are obviously more comfortable in class. I think it's because they live on campus and seem to know the professors quite well. They know each other because they live with the other students. They have access to study groups on the campus. They can get together and share. But for people like me who don't live on campus and can't get out at 9:00 or 10:00 p.m. and talk to our classmates to share notes and ideas, it's hard.

Then a lot of the stuff that they are teaching in my courses I've never heard of before. And the traditional students have already been exposed to it 'cause it doesn't seem to come as a shock to them. So I have to do a lot of outside reading. A lot of it, I'm sure, has to do with my background. It boils down to the fact that they are recent high school graduates as opposed to being in my situation. I have been out of high school for over twenty years. You're talking about a big difference here.

There have been times when I thought I was the only person lost. Then another student told me that she had panicked once with this same teacher. She told me she turned in a blank essay booklet and instructed the teacher to just fail her. I said to myself, "Someone is worse than me." I stuck it out and got a B.

I've had a serious problem with taking notes. In the beginning, I was trying to write down everything the teacher said. I would walk out of class with ten pages of notes and I noticed that the younger students would only have two or three pages of notes. I knew that there was a technique. There's a method to everything and if you don't know the secret you're in trouble. And most of the time, I'm in trouble. I'm getting a lot better though. I feel pretty good about it too.

I've participated in a few study groups and they have been helpful. However, it's a matter of getting invited into the group. One Sunday I was in the library and stumbled across a study group from my class. They invited me to join them. I think they felt that they didn't have a choice since I sort of asked. Mostly though the students stay away from me.

There was one teacher in a communications class who would judge students harshly, as if it were an English class. She'd put red marks all over my paper. It was hard making it in this class because I'd have to stand up in front of twenty strangers and deliver a speech. In that class I was the only minority, the only older student and the only Black student. The teacher tried to approach me and get me out of my shell, but it was clear that she saw me as just another young student. When it was time for me to give one of my final speeches, I had car problems and missed class. She gave me a zero, explaining that she had a strict policy about students missing their scheduled activities. I later found out that another student had wanted to give her speech that day and offered to take my place. But the professor had refused and instead dismissed class early. This really ticked me off. I was boiling. I explained to her that she couldn't treat me like the typical young college student. She reminded me of her strict policy. I told her that she would have to weigh how the lives of older students affect their schooling. I explained that I didn't live on campus and that getting to class for me was not a matter of just walking across campus. She eventually reconsidered and gave me the opportunity to give my speech. We had to come to an understanding that we were both adults. She had to understand that I was not a child.

There's Support and Then There's Support

My husband has been my number one supporter. He's a very bright man and realizes the importance of an education. He's in school working on his master's. He makes the 200 mile commute twice a week. So when he's gone, the kids and I eat out. I don't have to cook unless he's home. When he's home I will cook or my daughter will cook, or we will get in there and cook something together.

He makes straight "A's" and makes me want to go on. He sees something in me that I don't see in myself. I lack self-esteem. He seems to think that I can do whatever I want to do. He has really been a great motivator for me. He thinks I'm competent.

My family really supports me. It seems to make my daughter and son feel good when I study. Then at other times, if my studying interferes with their lives, they want me to stop and run them all over town. At other times they act as if they are not getting enough attention. So I block out time for them especially on the two days a week when my husband is gone. It's interesting that they don't interfere with my husband's study time. I don't understand why. Maybe it is because I spend more time with them than he does.

Another son who lives out of state is a great inspiration also. When I feel like I want to throw in the towel, with school, husband, and the whole deal, my son comes through for me. He always tells me that I can handle it. He says it makes him feel good to see both of his parents in school. I'm his stepmother and he was fourteen when he came to live with me and his dad. He excelled in our home and now he encourages me to go on and not give up. He says that my belief in him is what got him through college and now he's returning the favor. I remember that when he was stressed out in school and wanted to quit, I'd tell him to write down his thoughts. He now reminds me to do the same.

I feel real proud to be a student. I'm stumbling on ground to which my sisters and brother don't have access. When I finish I'll be the first college graduate out of my immediate family. This is really for my mother too. This is an accomplishment for me considering where I came from. It's quite an opportunity for me to be in any college, let alone being in this exclusive school. And I'm not having to work my way through college. And I'm still maintaining a household. It gives me peace of mind that I'm not having to borrow money to go to school and won't have to pay Uncle Sam back for my education. I am blessed.

Things Have Changed Around Here

People tell me that I'm doing very well, but maybe they are just telling me that to make me feel better. I'm trying to get over this hurdle in my life. I wonder what I'm capable of even when I'm succeeding. I don't want to let pride and overconfidence make me fall short of my goal.

My husband feels that I've really grown since I started school. He thinks I'm more open minded. I know this definitely has to do with college. College has really opened my eyes to a lot of women's issues, even though some of them don't relate to Black women. White women are put on a lower level than their men. This stratification in our society also puts White women in a position over Black women in terms of which group has power over which group. My way of looking at the world, especially how women live their lives, has changed. I used to always have dinner on the table and have my husband's clothes washed, folded, and in his drawers. Since I've been back in school, he's noticed that the wash was not getting done. I told him that he knew how to operate the washing machine. He's sharing more of the household chores now. And he's done all this without an argument. I told him that we were both in school and that I didn't have anymore time than he had. He understands about school though because he has his bachelor's degree.

When I go home to visit my mother I see a lot of people that I went to school with. I see the ones who had something going on, the ones who started out in college and never got through, the ones who've had two or three bad marriages. They remind me of how much they liked and admired me. I don't remember it that way. They say to me that I haven't changed. And I'm like, "Don't try it. All the hell that you gave me in high school and now I've made it and you won't acknowledge it. But that's okay. I know I've come a long way."

The circumstances of Beth's life placed college out of her reach. But she never gave up on wanting to achieve more. She started by making small steps and setting readily attainable goals—secretarial school and continuing education classes. While Beth credits so many others with supporting her, she seems unaware that she has been her own best support. Despite all the naysayers Beth never gave up on herself. She cared enough for her hopes and dreams to walk away from an unsatisfactory marriage. Eventually, when she sought a new rela-

tionship, one criterion was that her new mate value the benefit of an education. As she helped her husband and children succeed in school, Beth took note of their study habits and learned from their mistakes and successes. When an opportunity came along for her to attend college, she spoke up and took advantage of the opportunity. She has never questioned that decision.

CHAPTER 6

Faye:
No Babies on the Beach

Struggle in the face of blatant discrimination dominates Faye's story. This high-powered school board executive goes it alone and expects that the world will always see her as different. She carried these demons with her into an all-White university. Faye's story possesses answers and lessons for all nontraditional women who are returning to environments where they feel different and isolated from traditional college students.

Introduction

Faye, a forty-year-old school board administrator, is tall and erect in comportment. She is commanding not only in size but her mannerisms and style seem larger than life. This statuesque, full-figured woman has dark smooth skin, a short hair style that barely frames her face, big bold gold jewelry, and long abundant scarves that embrace her shoulders. Although her voice is soft and melodic, her presence dominates a room. Her manner and language relate that she is used to public appearances. She is skilled at intellectual discourse, seems constantly aware of her audience, and always controlled our interview process.

She attended segregated schools through the eighth grade until her parents forced her to be one of several Black girls to integrate a local White all-girls high school. She took a deep breath and exhaled before recounting her high school days. Faye then said curtly that, "It was difficult." School had always been one of Faye's favorite pastimes, and it was her straight "A" average that convinced her parents to volunteer her for the integration experiment. Although she was an above average student, she felt that no matter how hard she tried in this new environment her work was unfairly judged as "not quite good enough." After a traumatic four years of sometimes being ignored and oftentimes being taunted, she stated that she needed an all-Black experience in order to recover and retain her sanity. Faye attended a historically Black college for her undergraduate degree and a Northern Ivy League institution for her master's. She had recently finished her specialist's degree when we reviewed her reentry experiences.

Faye's interview was difficult to schedule because her calendar was crowded with speaking engagements and seminars that she does for the local school board and with operatic performances as part of a local quartet. Our interviews usually occurred after 10:00 p.m. on Friday nights. Often she was still dressed in her work clothing, variations of conservative blue suits and pumps. Our conversations seemed more like work sessions. Faye, because of her administrative background, constantly answered questions by giving me a systemic analysis of the situations. Her answers went beyond my questions and often included a societal examination of the issue. But all her intensity is framed in an elegant, genteel manner reminiscent of the mythical Old South and of bygone charm school days.

An eternal optimist, Faye sees life as a series of interlocking events and believes that many tragedies masquerade as opportunities in disguise. She sees all of her past life events as preparing her nicely for her return to school.

My experiences since I came back to school have been good. Basically I'm a lifetime student who loves school. My grades have always been good. As a minority, I did not encounter the prejudiced overtones because I knew everyone in the department at my university. I had encountered most of them in my official capacity as the curriculum director for a local school system. So just doing my job had exposed the professors to my capabilities as a student. Most understood my objectives and goals and knew that I was committed to achieving what was asked of me. My career provided me with a network, an experiential base (she was working in administration and pursuing a degree in administration), and a research agenda. I could talk about assignments that we were working on and a lot of times the professors would be in my school system providing services through my office. They (the professors) knew more about me than other first timers in the class or program.

But my situation is different, or should I say much better, than the circumstances of other minority students. Until there is a chance for minorities, Black folk in particular, to demonstrate their abilities I think that a question mark registers subconsciously in Black/White relationships. It's like, "Until we get to know you . . . " For minorities, it's a proving ground. It's hostile to you when you're the only one. Till all the flags are flown and the sign is given, minorities are fair game. What I mean is that it's easier for us to lose.

Faye steadfastly believes that only exceptional students of color receive fair treatment. She learned through observing classroom dynamics that the "run of the mill" student, especially Blacks and Black women, do not receive the benefit of the doubt.

If a Black student is in class and you are shy or you don't have an aura of enthusiasm, they will lose out. Many Blacks lose out this way because they fail to establish a comfort zone in their new settings—for themselves and for others who are not used to dealing with Blacks. A shy Black student will not be given the consideration that a shy student of another ilk will get. If a Black is not verbal or sociable, they are in trouble. When students divide into groups, if you look like you can contribute, you will get a chance. If a Black woman is quiet and misses that first chance, the other class members will probably not wait for her or consider her again. There are no babies on the beach.

Faye believes that intuition is a reentry student's best friend. Trusting in what she feels in her soul and remembering life lessons from previous experiences has kept her from making mistakes that befall younger students. She believes that no matter how much education you get, your instinct is never wrong. According to her, that little voice may seem irrational, but it is usually based on stored information that you are just not accessing. She knows that it was this gut feeling that led her to her present school.

I enrolled in two institutions to start my six-year degree. I went to one university and didn't like the overtones at the orientation. At the reception the professors acted as though they were afraid to talk to me. You were greeted at the door and then they didn't speak anymore. I said, "No way." Then the opening statement from the chair of the department sent vibes that convinced me that I was in the wrong place. He said that the program had a level of expectation that I might not be able to reach. That was a negative. I felt like if I had been successful in three graduate institutions all across this country, I wasn't going through those games. I went to another school the next day. The other campus was quite different. There was a sense of welcome. At the reception, they touched base with everyone in the room. I had a friend who stayed in the other program. As we compared notes about the style of the two programs, her experiences were miserable. Mine were better.

I Learned the Rules Early

When integration took place, I was in the first group to go to the White high school. I was scared. You already know before you go that there's something different about you. You already know that the rules may not be the same and that you might be rejected because of your skin color. The whole thing was mind boggling. I was the only Black girl in my class. There were ten of us (Blacks) in a high school of 400 who volunteered to integrate the school. Except I didn't volunteer. My parents volunteered me. We were a definite minority.

We, all four girls, were 4.0 students until we went there. My negative experiences included being left out of help sessions even when you'd ask for assistance. The discrimination was blatant. I'd watch as the teacher would give extra help to those that had asked. She would recognize that I was struggling, but wouldn't help. When I would ask a question the response might be something like, "You should have listened." But that was never the response to others. So a lot of times other students (Whites) who empathized would explain what the teacher had told them in the private help sessions. They would make apologetic statements like, "Heck, I didn't understand either. I don't know why she wouldn't explain it to you again."

After four years at the predominantly all-White girls school, for my undergraduate degree I went to a predominantly Black school for the respite. For my advanced degree, I again found myself in a mostly White environment. By then, I had the attitude that I was here to learn. I can do it. There was something inside of me that said I had something to prove. And I had my internal statement, "Yeah, I'm Black, but I'm not ordinary. I can do it."

I didn't allow myself to be trapped because when I decided to go to school I didn't go there to fit a mold. I went to get an education. I set out with a plan. I learned the rules early. I learned them the hard way.

Faye never forgets a rule once she learns it. As a life-long habit, she studies each new environment she enters in an effort to smooth her transitions and in order to play the game well. Faye feels that each new circumstance has a culture that she must learn in order to survive and prosper. Her current college setting is not entirely new to her. She has routine dealings with her teachers through her job with the local school board. Although she knows many of her professors in a professional capacity, she thinks that this advantage occasionally comes back to haunt her.

The Unwritten Rules

There was a Black friend in one of my classes. It was a professional relationship. She used to tell me quite often that she was not a writer. Once the professor asked me to work with her on her writing and make suggestions like, "Be more careful about typographical errors or grammatical usage." I felt that this was inappropriate and that he was seeking me out since we were friends. He was uncomfortable saying those things to her because she was Black. He didn't want to be perceived as a racist. I think teachers have an obligation to speak specifically to students about their shortcomings. Messages should not be carried to other students about the quality of another student's work.

This happens to me even in my staff development work for the board of education. For instance, I have a counseling project and three or four days ago

I got a call that four students were being dropped from the project. All four were Black and were being released because their delivery of work was insufficient and the quality was poor. I interrupted with the question, "Has it been brought to their attention?" And the response was, "No. At this level (a six-year degree program) they should know how to deliver a quality project." But how were they to know that they were performing poorly if they had not received adequate feedback or had not been given suggestions for improvement. It's just you go to class, you discuss, you work in small groups, and all of a sudden you are evaluated.

Well I believe that an educational setting should be designed to teach and work with those who do not understand although I know that some people, Black and White alike, enter programs without the capability to do the work. If that is the case in this situation, okay. But as explained by the students, they had done all that was required and had not received any feedback. Most of us have the capacity to learn what is shared.

I also recognize that there are varied levels of synthesizing that information and of being able to restate that information objectively whether it's test or dialogue discussion. It would be presumptuous of me to assume why the professor acted in the way that he acted. I talked to each one of these students on a one-on-one basis and it was disturbing that none of them knew that they were failing the class. The common threads were I turned in all the assignments; he never told me I was not doing well; I was an active participant; and I didn't know. In the end the professor said to them, "I've enjoyed having you in class. You should expect your grades soon." Yet, even more bizarre, none of these students challenged that professor's methodology or instructional model. I don't want to be that kind of student.

Faye shifts to an analysis of the students' roll in determining their own fate. Her comments speak directly to the silence and passivity found among disenfranchised students, such as older women students. While she is speaking only of her personal experiences and is making broad generalizations, studies done on women and minority students suggest that these students are socialized in their daily experiences to be quiet and docile. This style of relating to the world translates into a way of behaving in the classroom. It can directly impact students' interactions in group settings and the manner in which students relate to the professor and the curriculum.

It's been my observation not only in the work of education but even in community functions, Black folks don't ask questions. When I've taught and existed in predominantly Black settings, I found myself having to pull questions out of adults and children. It concerns me when people receive knowledge without questioning it. When I taught and worked in predominantly White settings, this was not true. I don't care what you teach, it's "Why?" or

"Do you know more?" or "Tell me more." I spend a whole lot of time telling people to ask questions.

Historically, we've been encouraged to be quiet. We've been raised not to ask questions. "Shut up and it might work out all right." This training came out of the circumstance of our existence, the olden days. So even now, I find this generation still not prone to ask questions, or to go the extra step to investigate. When people are raised to ask questions it does not put them in a position of appearing blatantly rude. They get answers and I think they go a lot farther than those that take the dish that's given to them.

In higher ed I believe that there are certain ways you have to ask questions if you are a minority or a woman. Professors appear more receptive if the challenge or inquiry is one of, "I need to know a little more. Would you help me please?" When the inquiry is pleading, it works, but if the point of inquiry is to test the knowledge base of an instructor then you usually meet with resistance. Usually what I've observed is that when Whites, especially males, doubt or dispute information, the professor will say something like, "Well there could be later research on that information. I would be interested in knowing more about it. Can you locate that?" But for a Black or a woman I have seen them become defensive. It's like, "You don't know more than I know. This is a fact. This is the way it will be done." And so in fact Blacks and other minorities usually do what they have been trained to do—and that's to step back and give others room. For those that don't step back the situation becomes that minority students are complicated individuals or that they are hard to get along with. Often the minority student is not the trouble. The minority student is just troubling the system.

Sometimes for safety's sake, especially when you know that you need the class or that there are specific goals, you say to yourself, "This too shall pass." You sort of conform. You do whatever you have to do to get out of the class.

I've been in many of those scenarios where things are said that were blatantly unfair and racist. For instance there was a class discussion where it was said that most Black folks can't swim because they aren't buoyant. I had to take a deep breath. Some Black folks don't swim because they haven't been taught and don't have the money to buy swimming pools or to go to the beaches or places where you swim. I grew up in an area where all public pools were for "Whites Only." Many people my age who grew up in segregated America had the same experience of limited or no swimming facilities. For Blacks living around the water, they swim pretty well. They usually don't need instructions and probably don't know what buoyant is, but they swim. Statements like that sometimes make me quiver. I think one would readily recognize that it has nothing to do with an individual being buoyant; it's about training people how to swim and having places for them to swim. In situations like that I have to speak up.

As a decision maker and as someone who is often in a position to provide training opportunities to correct such thinking, the first thing you have to do is to listen. It's also incumbent upon professionals to be fair and truthful. It doesn't matter whether you agree or not. Maybe it's that it doesn't matter about your prejudices. Your prejudices don't matter. I often ask myself, "How does that make you feel?" I felt squeamish. My judgment is based on whether there is a right or a wrong to the situation. If I believe that I can do something to correct it—yeah, I speak up. Sometimes though a situation can appear to be about race and it's not. It's about faulty thinking.

There are many situations where survival is the key. Race may seem the issue, but it's economics. Well, like once in curriculum we were talking about whether or not "Black English" should be taught. I didn't get upset because I have very definite views on something like that. I feel that whether it's Black English or Japanese or Chinese, or any other ethnic group's language or dialect, the languages are fine. But our economic base is drawn on the King's standard English language, so speak it. If you would like to have the quality of life that other folks have, then you say what you want to say at home, but at school and at work, you need to conform. In order to communicate and inevitably survive, you must speak and write in standard English. It's an economic point of view.

Overall, Faye sees her reentry experience and higher ed in general through her administrative lens. She believes that things would be more equitable if everyone realized that it is a business. As such, she thinks that ethical business practices should dictate the actions of students and professors.

Professional ethics for adult students and professors should set the stage. Then it would only take rules to solve most problems. You could work through any issue with professionalism. If the world were perfect, it would be simple. But if you are in the middle of your program and something unfair happens and you really want to finish school, you think priorities. You don't want to do anything to jeopardize achieving your goals. It often comes down to a dozen of one and twelve of the other. Now a lot of folks aren't smart enough to wait until that goal is achieved to pull the rug. And for those folks they tend to suffer or blow out before getting a handle on it.

There are ways to handle things. There is a definite hierarchy in the classroom. The teacher is the power broker and has your future—at least 75 percent of your future in his or her hands—25 percent I think belongs to you. Students are set up in a hierarchy. Anyone that could be classified in that Anglo-Saxon category via skin pigmentation is on top. It depends on the region of the country as to how other ethnic representatives are handled. I believe it is up to you to up the ante. I would perceive this typical setting as one where I would have to work extremely hard, especially if the professor is not fair, because it could mean that if this is a class where grades are given and not earned the minorities are going to suffer.

Reentering Takes Determination

Not only am I a reentry student, but in my job as staff development coordinator for the board of education I work with reentry students, mostly women, Black and White. So many of them have not been encouraged or mentored to go for it by anyone. There's some internal force that says, "I might want to try this." They have come to this point because there's some inner something. I'd go so far as to say of all of the students I've seen reenter school, get higher degrees, and then move up in their careers, I know of only two or three Black women who were actually mentored. The ones who were coached actually made it through to key positions because they were told exactly what to do, how to prepare, even helped with practice interview sessions.

Most of the other women were strong whether coached, mentored, or whatever. And I've also found that Black women seem to step out on faith, if you will. They say, "I'm going to do this." There is almost an innate will. I don't even know if there is real terminology to say what I'm trying to say. The determination says, "I'm going to try anyway even if I don't succeed. Some of these women now have positions that they have attained by force of will. I've heard them say things like, "I always knew that I wanted to be a principal," or "I wanted to do something rather than just be a mama or a housewife." And most have said things like, "Even though I was poor and didn't know how I was going to make it, I was willing to give it a try." Even in the process of trying, if things got rough, including school, for those that succeeded I've heard them say, "I had this professor and I didn't do well in that class, but I didn't let that stop me." With issues that had a central theme of racism, they seemed to endure. It didn't seem to matter because the conscious goal was there.

Most of my reentry experience has been positive. I went through my six-year program and never gave grades a thought. I just worked. There are two memories that I carried away from my experience.

At the end of my program of study I received a letter to be inducted into an honor society. I started not to go because the university is so large I feel like a number. But I said, "Oh well. What the heck." I decided to go. I went alone. My husband even questioned me on this. I wanted to go just to see. When I got there, I was the only Black person. And it was like the plague had walked into the room. I could read the expressions, "Oh we have one that is that smart?" I was asked questions like, "Where are you from? You are from the South?" In fact an acquaintance of mine from a class was inducted at the same time. She said to me, "Oh I didn't know you made straight 'A's'?" I just said, "Yes."

Another defining moment came for me at the end of my program. I commuted back and forth to campus. It was a two-hundred mile round trip. In my last quarter, I had a head-on collision. I was on my way to school and a truck crossed the center line and ploughed into me. All I remember is approaching a blind spot at the top of a hill and then waking up in the hospital. Still I had to finish school. It was near the end of my last quarter in school and I was taking three classes.

Since I was confined to bed, I asked for permission to complete my projects at home. Two of my professors said yes, but one said no. There were only two more sessions left and we never did anything in his class. He was a B.S.er. But he said no. I could tell that he was of another generation and was not comfortable dealing with me for whatever the reason. He thought I was asking for something extra. I wasn't able to get back on the road again for quite some time and eventually had to replace the course. I lost the entire course credit. But I made it. School was an opportunity. It was a challenge. It was exciting and meaningful. And it is done!

Physical pain accompanied Faye on her reentry journey. It may be more accurate to say that triumph over pain has been a pattern in her story. She endured long work days, a two-hundred mile commute to school twice a week, and a tragic car accident. Shortly after we finished our series of interviews, Faye was diagnosed with breast cancer. Thankfully, it was a battle that she won.

Faye opened her story by saying that she was a lifetime student. Her description was more accurate than she imagined. Shortly after she finished her six-year degree, she returned to school to complete her doctorate. She is currently learning her new job as a school superintendent.

CHAPTER 7

Lynda:
Signing My Name with an X

Several years ago Lynda awoke paralyzed. This life-changing event was a cata-lyst that forced her to take stock of her life. She reflected on what was working in her life and on what was failing during her many months of recovery. When she was well again, she began to make choices that would make her happy. She gave up a "good paying job" that she hated, her civil service job, entered college, and lived on public assistance while completing her degree. Her story is one of hope. She overcame physical, emotional, and monetary challenges to attend school. She risked it all to achieve her degree.

Introduction

Lynda has a short, full crop of straight thick silver hair that frames her seri-ous face and it makes her appear older than her fifty-four years. A stocky five feet three inches, she moves slowly and deliberately. Lynda is a widow with four children: a twenty-nine-year-old daughter, a twenty-year-old son, and a set of eighteen-year-old fraternal twins (a boy and a girl).

She is pursuing a nursing degree at a small community college and she lives with her children and a grandchild in a rent-subsidized apartment in a bustling business district of the city. Two of her children attend the institution where Lynda enrolled. Her oldest daughter is in the same program with her.

Lynda spoke of school as a place she was going back to with a specific pur-pose. Like so many reentry women, she is in school with a single goal in mind and doesn't expect it to be fun. As the oldest of the eight women who are telling their school stories, Lynda grew up in the deep South with Jim Crow. She is battle scarred by unpleasant memories of segregation, and she continues to see the world through her childhood pain. She feels that the world is more open now, in

71

terms of what can be achieved by women and people of color. This optimism along with the belief that she is setting an example for her children has sent her back to school. Lynda began her story by relating how difficult it was for her to return to a place that was never safe. One of Lynda's life-defining moments occurred in proximity to her schooling. She told the story as the center piece of her narrative.

The Front of the Bus

My most traumatic memory of school occurred one day when I was on my way to school. I was around ten years old and I rode the city bus to school each day. *Her mother had taught her how to change buses and had always taken her to the back of the bus. But she had not explained to Lynda why she should sit in the back of the bus.* I sat in the front of the bus that day and I sat next to a young White girl. We (Blacks) were not supposed to sit in the front. Sitting next to a White person was even worse. I didn't think to do like I'd always done. I didn't go to the back of the bus. I sat at the very front of the bus. I didn't think anything was wrong with it, nor did the little girl that I sat next to. I didn't know that I couldn't sit next to another child. We rode the bus and talked all the way to Broadway. *This incident occurred in the segregated South in the early 1950s. Lynda's sitting in the front of the bus violated a city ordinance.*

Well there was a guy on the bus who had been in the service. He had been all over the world and so he knew that segregation was not right and that it wasn't this way everywhere. When people on the bus tried to bother us, he said, "Leave those two girls alone." I was a child. I didn't know what was going on.

At that time they had those walkie talkies so the bus driver radioed ahead for the cops to meet us. When I arrived at school my teacher, Mrs. Simons, and the principal, Mr. Thomas, were waiting for me. They had identified me as the little girl with the red raincoat. So when I arrived at my school the police had instructed Mrs. Simons and Mr. Thomas to get the girl with the red raincoat.

Mrs. Simons came and hugged me and said, "We have to take you down to city hall." First she took me to the office and sat with me explaining the struggles that Blacks were encountering. "Your mother and father are there. They know." I started crying and asking, "Why was I going to city hall? What had I done wrong?" She just hugged me and said, "You didn't do anything wrong. All you did was ride the bus to school." Somehow the other little girl's parents and the Whites on the bus made a big issue out of my sitting next to a White girl. I was very frightened and it was Mrs. Simons' words of assurance that carried me through. All I could hear was what she had said, "You will be alright Lynda. You didn't do anything wrong." We went down to City Hall. I missed an entire day of school. And after that experience it was inside of me as a child that there was a difference between Blacks and Whites and that they (Whites) didn't like Blacks. Yet I didn't grow up feeling resentful toward Whites, but I could have.

Lynda states that she will never forget the day she spent in court having to answer questions about her behavior. The grownups asked her about a situation that she still describes in a soft almost childlike voice as "innocent." She vividly remembers the hostile environment and the fingers pointed in her face. Years later, Lynda experienced a flashback when a colleague pointed her finger in her face. According to Lynda, she had trained a new employee only to discover that the new employee was to be her boss. Shortly after the employee assumed her supervisory duties, she confronted Lynda about a task that she felt Lynda had not successfully completed. Before Lynda could answer, the supervisor yelled at her and pointed her finger in Lynda's face.

She just walked up to me and put her finger in my face. I found myself in that courtroom again having to explain that, "I didn't do anything." I snapped. I almost choked her to death. When I was asked by our supervisor what had happened, I couldn't explain. But I knew then and there that this job situation was not for me. All I could think and I just kept repeating to myself, "Lord, we've (Blacks) had to go through so much. We are still going through so much. How much more, Lord? How much more?"

Lynda's answer to the question was, "Not much more." Life circumstances conspired to take her on a different path, one that led back to school.

A Time for Change: A Time for Me

One day I was sitting at my desk interviewing a client. Suddenly I was having difficulty moving. I thought that I was having a stroke. I called for my supervisor and told her that something was very wrong. She called for her supervisor, who got me to the hospital. As it turned out a vertebrae in my spine collapsed injuring a nerve on my right side. I had extensive damage to a major nerve in my neck and all the levels of my neck had to be reconstructed. The injury was the aftermath of an automobile accident that I had a year earlier. I had surgery immediately to fuse the vertebrae in my upper spine. When I woke up from the surgery I could not use the right upper side of my body and I could not speak. I did not think I was ever going to be able to talk or move about freely. But I kept praying and putting it in God's hands. I was not able to talk or write for a year. I had to sign my name with an X. I kept remembering that my grandmother could not read. She signed her name with an X. And now here I was signing my name the same way.

Lynda found herself relegated to the same disheartening conditions her grandmother had endured. At least, she reasoned, her grandmother had been able to talk. So she felt that she was in worse shape. She prayed day and night and thought about the irony of her situation. Finally, during her long hospitalization, in what she described as a very spiritual moment, she received her answer.

While I was flat on my back, I was not able to explain what I needed or wanted. I spent most of my time in the house crying and trying to realize why this had happened. From July through November I could not speak. I regained my voice right after Thanksgiving. I was able to go back to work the next January. I had worked in state government for twenty years. The job that I was in was just too stressful and it was time for me to see about Lynda. I turned it over and over in my mind trying to make a decision whether to go back to school or to continue working for the state. When I went back to work after regaining the use of my arm and voice, my job had been upgraded. The work was more difficult and the caseload was heavier. Since I had reached longevity in the state system, I had no real future. I was training people who were coming in making more money and who had more prospects. And I had promised myself in the months when all I could do was think and pray that I would go to college.

Just after I got back to work I was sitting at my desk and I said, "I know what I must do with the remainder of my life. I want to go to school. I like working with people. I've always wanted to work with kids. So I think it is time for me to do some of the things that I want to do."

I've always wanted to be an important Black woman in society. And I know that I need to go to college. My mother was not able to send me to college when I finished high school. She had saved for my college education, but she was persuaded to help her brother's children with my college money. She thought that later, when my turn came, her brother and his newly college-educated children would help me. When I was ready to go to college, my uncle and his family would not help. I resented them and my mother for a long time. Why did she devote so much time and my money to them? They had all finished school, but none of them offered to help. Eventually the Lord took that bitterness away. So I don't have any regrets from that because it made me desperate to be successful. And this drive has carried me through many situations.

Reentry: Completing the Circle

Lynda always dreamed of being a nurse. This desire was cemented by her role as family caretaker. Fifteen years ago she enrolled in the nursing program in which she is now currently registered, but she never showed up for class. She felt that she needed to continue working as a caseworker for the local Department of Family and Children Services for the good of the family.

In 1976 when I first enrolled in school I kept putting it off. I guess my husband felt that the timing was not right. He wanted to make sure that the kids were the priority. My husband was not supportive of my going back to school. He saw it as a way of moving away from him or of trying to grow beyond him. Shortly after I made the decision to return to school this time, we separated. Once we separated we never got back together. However, he did move back in when he found out that he was dying. I took care of him until he passed away. I'm glad that before he died he said, "I'm so sorry that I didn't see this before now. When you had the twins if I had listened and had let you go to school you would have been real successful."

The second time that I decided to return to school my children were old enough to have their say. Instead of being supportive, my children got angry when I told them I was going to quit my job and go to school. My son was in his senior year of high school and my twins were in the eleventh grade. They kept saying, "Mama how are we going to live? How are we going to do this?" And I kept saying, "There's a God. God will make a way for us." At first I don't think they understood. They thought I was being irresponsible. But I was not being irresponsible. I had money saved. I reminded them that even if I failed they had a father—even though we were separated. I guess they thought we'd end up outdoors, homeless. They kept thinking of all the things we would lose, not of what we would gain. And it was turmoil for me, but in the long run you know it has paid off for me. My kids are now more excited about me returning to school. Once they saw that I had a plan, they became supportive.

The dilemma that Lynda faced is the classic example of why so many reentry women defer the decisions to pursue a college education. Stories told by reentry women repeatedly state that the family is understanding and offers support as long as the mother's or wife's return to school and the subsequent demands of school work do not affect them financially or significantly interrupt the flow of the household.

For the True Good of the Family

Going back to school has been a wonderful experience and it's been an awful experience. One of the main reasons that I came back to school was to set an example for my children. I want them to know the importance of getting an education now. I don't want them to wait like I did. And if they can get the funding and financial aid then they should go. Back when I wanted to go on to college from high school, there were no financial aid programs. If there were, people like me did not know about them. Your family had to have the money if you wanted to go on to college.

Students in Lynda's age group, fifty and older, express this sentiment quite often. Their college years occurred before federal financial aid was available. In addition, Lynda's socioeconomic level affected her ability to pursue college. Knowing how to get a college education is information easily obtained by the middle-class but is not so accessible to the poor and people of color.

My oldest daughter was supposed to come out here to school, but she got pregnant. Her boyfriend disappointed her and wouldn't marry her. She put her school plans on hold. I sat down and talked to her, but I thought it would be better to show her. So one morning, I got up and she said, "Where are you going?" And I said, "I'm going to class," and I left. The kids who were living at home knew that I was in school, but my oldest daughter did not. I had informed her of my plans but I had not given her the details. She thought that I was only talking and would never actually go to school. I told her how this had been my dream, but that I didn't have the support. And I told her that just because she had made a mistake and gotten pregnant didn't mean she had to put off her schooling. She didn't have to repeat my mistake. I had been so concerned about taking care of my mother, grandmother, children, and husband, I didn't take care of myself. I had always put everybody else first instead of myself. The next thing I knew my daughter had moved back home, enrolled in school, and she's in classes with me.

Many reentry women with adolescent or young adult children say that the decision to return to school was made partially to inspire their children to also pursue a higher education. This again demonstrates how women incorporate the caretaker role into their lives even when following their own dreams.

When I first started school, I had to take developmental studies since I had been out of school for thirty-five years. But the woman who is the director of the program has been a great connection. She plays an important role for the Black students at this college. Since she's on the faculty, she knows the inside stories. There have been times when I thought I could handle a teacher or a course and she would say, "No you don't want to take that teacher for that class." Students will also warn you who you should stay away from because the teacher is unfair.

I work with the developmental studies counselor a lot. She has been my mentor. She's also the advisor for the student minority program and the Black Student Union (BSU). As the president of the BSU, I work with her and many of the Black students here at the college. Unfortunately, many of the students only come to the organization to take advantage of our services when there is a problem on campus. I am constantly telling them to be involved on campus. Don't let others discourage you from joining groups and attending activities. I had heard negative things about the BSU, but I decided not to listen and to observe for myself. Now I'm the president. I'm the oldest president that the organization has ever had. From time to time I have to intervene, along with the group's advisor, between a student and a professor. Usually it's (the conflict) about grades. We sit down and try to reason it out. I spend a lot of time doing student support services, getting students into study groups and setting up tutorial sessions.

It's been pleasant dealing with young people who are just coming out of high school. Looking at them, I realize that our kids (poor Black kids) have missed so much. It's sad. They don't have discipline. No one has cared for them. They don't realize the importance of their education. They don't realize the importance of their financial aid, their grants, their scholarships. And I've seen it taken away from them without a moment's thought. It is ridiculous. They sit around the game room and play cards all day. Then when they get a bad grade they come to organizations like the BSU (to say that they've been discriminated against). What they should realize is that the White kid is making the grade. If he is not making the grade, the professor may give him the benefit of the doubt. Whereas the professor will not give a Black student the same benefit of the doubt.

The Ups and Downs of School

Now the typical school day for me can be frustrating. It begins at home. I sometimes leave my materials laying out and my kids move my books so I have to run around and gather things up before I can leave for class. I don't drive since the surgery so my son or daughter take turns taking me to class. They are both students here. I always arrive to my classes on time because I don't like being late for class. I'll stay on campus from 8:00 a.m. until around 1:00 p.m.

It hasn't been easy. I've had to drop classes. I decided to get out of a computer class because I didn't know the new keyboard. I was doing real well in the class. I knew where the letters were, but then the instructor would say something like, "Give me a cursor." And I would wonder, "What is this lady talking about? What in the world is a cursor?" Finally it hit me that I was in the wrong class. I talked to her, but I dropped the class. I made sure that she understood that I was enjoying it, but that she was going too fast. She was assuming that I had knowledge that just didn't exist for me. When I was in school thirty-five years ago there was no cursor.

When I first came out here I really enjoyed it. Then there were too many of us (Blacks) and the school decided to do something to improve their image.

Now the number of Black students is low. It's just pathetic. They don't want us out here.

Even though all my life I wanted to be a nurse, this nursing program is so complicated—I'm ready to leave. I know that I could be elsewhere working on my B.S. and be through. Then if I want to go back to the nursing program, I could go somewhere else where Blacks are appreciated. Then I looked at the number of hours that I have and I looked at my credits and I reconsidered. But just walking through the nursing department and looking at the pictures of those who have graduated tells you a story. There are no Black students among the graduates. If someone would just look around, the answer is there. Black enrollment is down and continuing to fall because the students know that there is a problem here and that they are not wanted.

We've (Blacks) been fighting all our lives. We always have to prove ourselves. We always have to answer why we want to do this—why do you need this step. And you know the higher you go the more you've got to prove yourself. I want the same quality education that Whites have been getting all along. When I finished high school the opportunities were not there for Black women. The only thing that was open to you was teaching (in segregated schools). And so when other fields opened we went in and we've been successful. But the gates didn't just open easily. At the educational end, there are still certain instructors that will hold you back. I've gone to some of these teachers to ask, "Where did I make a mistake?" I can always tell the difference from those who want you to succeed and those who don't care. There have been teachers who have refused even to talk to me.

Lynda's scenario of dealing with "rusty" study skills or of having to face new materials is common among nontraditional college women. However, it is reassuring to know that once reentry women become accustomed to their new environment they perform much better than the traditional college student. They interact more frequently in the classroom and routinely report superior grade point averages.

When I first came out here I had a 4.0 average. Then I had a 3.0 average. Now, I think I'm at a 2.5. It has not been easy. Since I've been in school, my husband and my mother-in-law both died. I nursed and cared for both of them during their illnesses while I continued to attend school. I don't have any other family, brothers or sisters, who could have helped. So it's just been up and down as far as my school work is concerned.

If there is a negative bond shared by most reentry women, no matter the economic level, race, or ethnicity, it is self-doubt. Despite the burgeoning numbers of nontraditional college women and regardless of the common success stories found within this group, they continue to doubt their abilities. Unfortunately, they often wonder whether they fit in and whether they are as smart or as quick as the average college student. Reentry women are becoming the "average" college student. They appear smarter than their younger counterparts when grade point averages are compared. When told this, reentry women downplay the significance and attribute it to the wisdom and seriousness that come with age.

Sometimes I ask myself as a student if I'm out of place. Then I see that I am a mentor to other students. I'm amazed how the younger students approach me in the classroom. It makes me feel good because I guess they realize that I do understand the material. They will approach me and say, "Miss Lynda, did you get that?" Or they will ask me if they can help me if they see that I'm having problems writing something.

It seems that Lynda's school life has come full circle. Her favorite part of school in the elementary years was always the interactions with the other students. Even the teacher who greatly shaped her early school days recently told Lynda how proud she was that Lynda had returned to school. For Lynda, this was another indication that she had chosen the right path.

The teacher who pushed me to succeed, Mrs. Simons, is still someone that I feel a very close connection to. With her encouragement I felt that I could accomplish anything. I was her pet pupil and she was my favorite teacher. Just a month or so ago when I saw her she hugged me like she did the day I was arrested. She was glad that I was in school. She said that she always knew that I had the initiative, but that my family did not have the money.

Returning to school at fifty-four has given me the initiative to learn. Most of my classes have been okay and my instructors have been pretty much on top of things. I know that I can continue to learn. After my illness, I didn't think that I was capable of retaining knowledge, of holding the material that I had to learn. I thought my ability to learn had been impacted because my speech slowed so much as a result of my injury. As a result of my accident and surgery, I have processing problems. Sometimes I am not able to pick up everything that is on the board. But it hasn't slowed me down too much. My motor skills are not as fast as they once were and so I have difficulty taking notes in class. My hands can not keep up with my brain or the teacher's lecturing. In the beginning I didn't think that my memory was going to come back. But it has. When I first came back to school, I was completely lost. The fear controlled me. I'd say, "Oh my God I can't do this." One of the counselors realized that I was terrified. She gave me a set of recorded relaxation cassette tapes. I started listening to them before an exam and it worked. I don't go into a test anymore and say, "Oh Lord, I can't do this." Instead I get a good night's sleep and go for it. It has been the best method.

I still speak slower and there are words that I struggle with even now. I have two dear friends, older students, a White woman and a Black man, who work with me on pronouncing the more complicated biology terms. He especially won't let me get away with saying, "I just can't do it." Older students seem to find a way to make up for whatever deficiencies we have. We are more serious. It has been like a dream for me to be able to return to school and to be successful in my classes. I have not failed a class. At my age this schooling experience is one of the greatest gifts that I have encountered.

After a lifetime of putting her goals on hold for others, Lynda decided to go full steam ahead toward a two-year degree in nursing. Pursuing her education inconvenienced her children and other family members, but Lynda felt that their comfort had been her priority for much too long. Her illness taught her to see her health and well-being as precious gifts. And she decided that at fifty-four it was now or never. School for Lynda, as for many reentry women, was one of the major objectives left undone. And being able to reflect on its importance during the imposed silence of her paralysis helped her to promise anew that this time nothing would deter her from her nursing degree.

CHAPTER 8

Sheila:
Turn Off the Light

During her fourth attempt to return to college for an undergraduate degree, Sheila struggles with a husband who hates how her school schedule and homework interfere with his home life. As Sheila studies into the early morning hours, his constant mantra has become, "Turn off the light. Come to bed." In this chapter, the issues of family conflict are explored.

Introduction

Sheila is a thirty-eight-year-old student at a large southeastern research university. She has returned after a fourteen-year hiatus and is attempting to finish her undergraduate degree. She has stepped away from her education several times. During her first tenure at this school (the second university she has attended), she dropped out after the first quarter because balancing school and a new marriage was too difficult.

 She lives about five miles from the university and must pass through or go near the campus daily. Living in the shadow of the university constantly reminded her of unfinished business—that undergraduate college degree. Sheila, a first-generation college student, attends school on a college stipend. A psychology major, she intends to teach disabled children upon graduation. A woman of medium height, five feet five inches, with a small compact muscular build, Sheila maintains a formal and quiet presence. She has a coffee-cream-colored flawless complexion and wears her dark brown straight hair shoulder length and swept away from her face. She smiles easily, but does not laugh often. Her eyes are expressive but convey that she is tired. Her rigorous schedule includes full-time employment as a teacher's aide at a psycho-educational center and a full-time college schedule.

School Is Like . . .

If I had to compare school to something, I'd say it was like an upset stomach. It's like bubbles in your stomach especially at those times when you haven't put as much time into it as you need. It is so stressful. It is a disaster. It worries me. I'm constantly thinking, "Have I done this? I know I have to do something else." It's like having a nervous stomach, a headache, a tense body, with no relief. On days like that I spend the whole day knowing that I need to study for a test but how can I? *Sheila describes a life with little rest. Many reentry women state that they realized that school would be a new experience that would require a reshuffling of their schedules. Many women who return to school overwhelmingly lament that school has become an additional obligation that has been piled on to other family and personal obligations.*

Up at seven. At one time I was getting the baby dressed. I would find myself being late. Like thirty minutes, sometimes fifteen, late for work. So right after Christmas I started getting myself dressed and letting my husband get the baby dressed. I feel better now that I go to work on time, at eight o'clock. It's at work that I get to sit down and think about what I have to do when I leave work. When my work day ends, I'll pick up my daughter and take her to piano practice. And on those days that she doesn't go to piano practice I get off work and go pick up the baby (a one-year-old girl) and have her home about 4:14. My class starts at 4:30. So it's rush, rush, rush. When I leave that class around 6:00 p.m., I go straight to another class, Monday through Thursday. Finding parking places when I first get to campus is almost impossible. Then I have to try to find another parking place for the second class, all the while trying not to be late for class.

Sheila describes a school life full of complexities not faced by traditional students. According to her, it's the little things like driving to the campus and finding a parking place rather than just walking over from the dorm or catching the bus to class. Reentry women find that although their numbers are increasing in the university and college communities, the environment is not adapting to them, but instead expects them to change their lives to fit the traditional college format. Routinely they face trying to reschedule their "real" lives of work, children, and family obligations, in order to register for classes, meet with professors, or attend special lectures or events on campus during the day.

Sheila's life is no exception. After a day that begins at seven in the morning, she returns home around 8:30 p.m. She sandwiches most of the housework and child care responsibilities between studying. On an average homework-filled night, she goes to bed between 2:00 and 4:00 a.m.

Most days after school, I go home, make sure the kids are okay, prepare meals, and study. It's a constant grind of tidying things up so that you can make your way through them, and catch up. I try to study, but I don't feel comfortable sometimes in my own home trying to study. A lot of nights I try reading in bed but my husband is trying to sleep and he wants quiet and darkness. My husband doesn't understand. He has never been to college. He doesn't understand what it takes. So we argue. He always says, "Turn off the light. How long are you going to study?" He is not too accepting of all the things I have to do for school.

I try to study in other parts of the house, but he comes and tells me to come to bed. Leaving home to study is something I don't feel comfortable doing. I wish I could maybe go to the library. Yet I know it's my fault that I don't carve out any real time or have any real space where I can study. It's not that I haven't thought about it or tried it. I just want to be with my family. But I can't study efficiently or properly the way things are now. It will have to change. For right now that's kind of a struggle. It's very hard trying to find an appropriate place to study.

While Sheila tries to find time to study, she also feels she's an isolated student without support. This sense of isolation affects her schooling. She feels that being in a large university setting where she doesn't know anyone is hard especially when she is faced with a difficult assignment or subject, like math. Now well into her second year of this undergraduate sojourn, she has never been part of a study group nor made any college friends. She describes the reentry experience as a singular one. She has sought help from her church and community in order to remedy her need for a study partner or group.

When I need extra help with school work I find people outside of college to tutor me. It's so hard to make an appointment with a professor or to get tutoring on campus because of my work schedule. It's inconvenient. You have to make appointments during regular school hours when they are available. That's when I'm working. I try to explain this to professors, but my schedule doesn't matter to anyone but me. Other than work hours, the only time that I could be tutored is between 4:00 and 7:00 p.m. and that's when I'm in class. I found a church member who was willing to tutor me in math. He is a high school math teacher. He's been great. I feel guilty about taking his time from his family. I know that he's also missing his weekend TV football games. But thank God he tutors me. He remembers what it was like since he went back to school as an adult.

I don't really have any contacts at school, no one to study with, or no one to call when I'm out of school. The closest I've come to having any support has been the singing group. There's a group on campus that sings Negro Spirituals and Gospel songs. Since I've joined, it kind of helps me along. It makes me want to continue school. And I couldn't afford to take the chorale classes. If you sign up for the classes I would have to pay full tuition. Right now I'm registered as an evening student. The classes for the chorus are in the daytime and are for regular students. They cost more. If I split my schedule, it would be more money. My academic assistance will only give me so much. I have to use it the best way that I can. The group's director has let me participate on a volunteer basis. I like being a part of the group because it is uplifting. It makes a difference in my life and my studies. We sing inspirational songs. And I learn fascinating details like, Martin Luther King's favorite song was "Battle Hymn of the Republic." Singing with this group has become a form of prayer for me. And I need something to get me through.

Guilt seems to pervade Sheila's story. She casts the domain of the home as entirely her charge and appears grateful for any assistance from her spouse and child. So many women who have children in the home speak in guilty tones of shifting more responsibility on to their children, rather than to their partners or husbands. What is apparent in many of the examples given by Sheila and by others is that the bulk of the obligations are placed on female children. She feels bad that school takes her away from her family and that she cannot perform all the household chores that she once handled.

Even though I'm in school, I still have to come home and do almost everything. My daughter, who is thirteen, really tries to help. She washes the dishes. When she goes to wash the dishes I feel guilty so I'll go in the kitchen to help her. It's not her job. She has homework. I want her to get her homework done 'cause the dishes will get done eventually. So if I help her it moves faster. I will just collect everything and pile stuff up. Then she will wash them. Then I might come back and dry them.

My husband helps some. He is supportive in his own way. He prepares some meals. He cooks, mostly his dinner. He washes clothes, mostly his. And he is home when I'm away at school. He makes sure that the kids are home. He supervises them until I get home. I'm not knocking it. It's a help. But it's not a good feeling for me that my husband is not doing more. I just try not to labor on that fact. I try to concentrate on what I have to do. If I stopped long enough to let that get me down I wouldn't continue to do what I've set out to do: finish school. So I'll stay up sometimes till 4:00 a.m. Then I go to work at 8:00 a.m. dragging. This has gotten to be my routine. It's exhausting. It's killing me. There really isn't anyone that I can talk to about this.

When we sat down to talk for the second time, Sheila had reached a critical point in her schooling. She was questioning why she was in school. Was she doing it for her grandmother, her daughter, or herself? And she was wondering whether it was all worth it. Her dilemma is one faced by so many reentry women as their dream of school becomes the reality of a schedule that is unrelenting.

What Does My Example Mean?
What Are My Actions Saying?

It's important for me to earn this degree because I think of how it will change my life. I think about my children and how moving up in my job will benefit them. I am definitely planning for them to attend college. I know that the insurance that we have for their college education is not going to be enough. My husband, who is only forty-six, is planning on retiring soon. He has been on his job long enough to retire even though he is not near sixty-five. He's planning on quitting work and letting the family live off my salary. And my paycheck won't amount to anything if I'm making what I'm making now. So I think that financially, it is very important that I get a college education.

One of the reasons that I came back to school was because a co-worker made me realize that I was working as a teacher and being paid as an aide simply because I didn't have the credentials. I'm doing the same amount of work as people who are getting paid twice as much.

I think I'm also back in college to set an example for my daughters. My oldest daughter wants to be a teacher now. She says, "Mama, you're a teacher now aren't you? You're not an aide are you? You're a teacher, aren't you?" So she is supportive. But sometimes she will be the child that she is and resent having to take care of her younger sister. She'll say, "This is your baby. You need to come get your baby and keep it." It's really hard having a baby at home who can't do for herself. When I came back to school she was one year old. She's two and she's putting everything in her mouth, putting things up her nose.

My grandmother was another reason that I wanted to come back to school. She had a third-grade education. But she had the wisdom and the knowledge as far as getting along with people. I inherited that from her. She wasn't a big socializer. She stayed at home and took care of home. She didn't run from this house to this house. She didn't let me rip and run the streets. She was strong. I remember her saying that she only sent me to school to get a high school education. She thought that was enough. She thought that was a big thing. I don't think it was the way it could have been if I had my biological parents raising me instead of my grandparents. The reason I feel this way is because I want things for my children that I didn't have. And my grandmother only wanted so much for me. I think she thought it was enough, but I don't think parents would have thought it was enough. She only knew so much. It's all she knew. It could have been better.

There were some days that weren't so happy. I can remember going to school days without lunch money. I had to wash tables to eat. For some reason my grandmother thought that when you got home you got a chance to eat as much as you wanted, so why eat at school. It embarrassed me for a while, but there was a pay off. I knew that there was no such thing as a free lunch.

Another time that was embarrassing was when I reached puberty and my body was changing. I started perspiring. I didn't know I needed to start wearing deodorant. The teacher gave me powder and stuff to put under my underarms. I didn't let my grandmother know. I didn't know how to tell her. I just went and hid it in my closet.

Once while going through the lunch line the principal asked me, "Did you comb your hair?" She (my grandmother) thought it didn't need combing . . . brushing was okay. It made me kind of sad. Just little things like that could have made my life more pleasant. I hate to say bad things about my grandmother.

She did the best she knew how to do. I love her to death. No one in my family has ever been to college. I had an uncle who had a year of college and that was because he played football. I needed to show her that I could do it. But before my grandmother died she was senile. She didn't know me anymore, let alone know that I was in school. Yet I know at the same time that she wanted whatever was beneficial to me. She would be proud of me still because it is something that I want to do. I remember when we talked about it once she said, "If this is something that you really want, go and get it. I will help you anyway that I can. I don't have any money to give you but if you want me to keep the baby just bring her over." She gave me what she had to give. I had to ask myself if I was doing this for me or for her. Now I'm clear that college is just for me and my self-gratification.

Sheila recalls her home life with her well-meaning grandmother as mostly work and loneliness. There were, however, good times. The happy memories are connected to opportunities that school can provide both directly and indirectly. That memory is part of what has brought Sheila back to school.

My best memories of school are of traveling with the basketball team when I was in the ninth grade. I got a chance to go places where I'd never been before. In junior high it was an all-Black team and we occasionally got to travel with the high school team which was quite an experience. It was back when girls played half-court ball. You had three girls on one side of the line and three on the other side. We used to carry the ball to the line and pass it over to the girls who were the shooters.

It was kind of fearful traveling around the South. The older ones would tell jokes on the bus about the danger involved. They'd say, "Now y'all be careful in this place because they don't allow y'all (Blacks) up here in this part of the state." But it was interesting seeing how others lived. Some of the incidents that stick out in my mind involve the strange meals we were served after the games. Once we were served grits. I remember thinking that no matter how poor we were even we didn't eat grits for dinner.

Traveling was an opportunity that I didn't have except for sports. But my older child, we take her places so she sees a lot. I didn't have anybody to take me places. And being in those organizations was my way out of the South. Even for a little while. If it was just for an hour or two, I got a chance to see some things. That was exciting.

School in a way was my salvation. There were a couple of teachers from those days who were role models. They helped me along the way. One of them, a Black woman, would have me over to help her clean the house. It was her way of giving me money. The other teacher, a White woman, took me to visit the first college that she attended. She still keeps in touch and encourages me to go ahead and finish college. When she heard that I was back in college, she called me to tell me that she was glad that I was back. She also came to my grandmother's funeral and gave me a card with money in it to help out with my college expenses. She wanted to know how school was coming. She has become a lifelong friend.

I think back on those times (the segregated school days) and how different it was when the schools integrated. We went from eating grits to eating steaks. We had two or three uniforms. We rode greyhound buses instead of school buses. We ate before and after the games. It was just different. And you know what? I liked the segregated times just as much as the integrated times because they both offered special things.

After integration, looking back on it now, I guess I realize that my self-esteem was kind of low. When we were segregated I got the chance to sing in a school play. That was very special for me. After integration they didn't have different plays. Those extra activities were just cut out. It became like high school, just academics. Outside of class there was no reason for the students to mix. If you wanted to shine, you had to be in sports. Academically you had to be an "A" student to be popular or you had to be a basketball or football player. It was hard to make it in the new environment because the help was no longer there. There were no concerned teachers or school officials to make sure you got extra help if you needed it. Only one Black person that I know of ever got honors—straight "A's"—after integration.

As the years went on you didn't get a chance to shine or glow or stand out because there were so many people either smarter than you or who had certain talents that stood them apart. I didn't get a chance to do little things that I loved to do after the schools were integrated.

You Never Know What You Might Become After You Get a Degree

Well I had attempted to come back to college on several occasions. The first year when I left high school I wanted to go to college. I didn't want to get out straight into the working field. So I went to a small predominantly Black state college and stayed there a year. I enrolled at this university for Summer School and thought I would try to make it here. I decided not to return to my first school and I dropped out of this university after my first quarter. Off and on I found jobs. By then I had met my husband and he said, "Why don't you go back and I'll help you." So after we paid the loans from the first year, I went back to school. The same year that I married I was back at the university. It was quite a challenge. It was like everything was over my head. I just couldn't see straight because my mind was not on school. I couldn't see studying and not understanding what was going on. Sure it would be nice to have a degree but my mind was not on school. I finally said, "No, I ain't' got time for this. This is just too much stress." So I said, "I'll just leave that alone." I said, "We can make it. You and I, we will make it together." It was stressful just trying to live two lives. It's like living the life of the student and living the life of a wife. So I decided to maintain my marriage and try to keep up with my husband.

After having had several jobs, plant work, managing a fast food restaurant, and selling Tupperware, Sheila sees school and the opportunities connected to it through different eyes. Sheila finally landed in a job that she felt could become a career, working at a psycho-educational center for children with developmental disabilities. The people she worked with made a tremendous impact on her life and career goals.

It was a chance meeting at my latest job at the psycho-ed center that led me back to school. One day after work a co-worker introduced me to a friend of hers. The friend said that she had heard wonderful things about me, how I helped her girlfriend with her psychology homework, how I could look at a child or just walk into a classroom and make a diagnosis, or know what the child needed, or know what would help the child improve. Every time she'd see me she'd say, "I've been hearing nice things about you. Why don't you go back to school?" I'd say, "Oh no, school is not for me. I can't go back to school. I don't know. I'm just as content as I am. I'm just going to continue to do what I'm doing." She kept saying, "Go back to school. You never know what you might become after you've gotten that degree."

And the fact that this one woman believed in me made me feel that I could do it. I finally said, "Okay. I'll try it." Even before I attempted to register for school she was talking graduation. She told me that anyone who can diagnose those kids like you, can get a college degree. You have it upstairs. It just motivated me to do it—to just attempt it one more time. Overall, the people that I work with have been a positive influence. When I want to leave to attend a tutoring session or leave early to register or if I need someone to proofread my paper, they are there. They encourage me to continue because most of them have graduated. They say just keep it up. Hang in there.

As a matter of fact, another reason why I did go back is because my life is more stable now. I'm secure at work and at home. And I felt that I could do it this time. My husband is more stable. He is a recovering alcoholic. And I felt that I had his support. He wanted me to finish what I had started. And I said well I do have a stable home right now. I reasoned that if he won his battle to stay sober, I could try to get my degree. I knew that if he could do that, I can at least try to finish school. When I returned to school he had been sober for two years.

Central to Sheila's story of school is a theme revealed in many accounts told by nontraditional women students—doubt. She often wonders if she's a good student. The lens through which she views her current life is one that was significantly shaped by a childhood of poverty. However, as she has worked to overcome these feelings, often she is trapped by unfair assessments. Sheila talked about a teacher who openly expressed negative stereotypical ideas about Blacks with her classroom stories.

This professor would just talk about things that she really didn't understand, things she didn't know about. As a psychology professor, she felt comfortable speculating about why people were fat or why Black people behaved in certain ways. And she would end every negative story about Blacks with a statement to me, "Now if I'm wrong, now speak up and defend yourself." She told this one story of her Black cleaning lady who had worked for several people and was usually fired for poor performance. But the professor explained that to her credit she did not fire the woman because she saw it as her duty to make this woman, who would never be more than a mere cleaning woman, a better cleaning woman. The professor explained that "these people" will never be successful at much if you don't make them do their simple jobs over and over until they get them right. In a way, she said that they were like "children."

Several weeks into the quarter, most of the Blacks in the class had dropped the course. Sheila felt trapped because she needed the course since it was the only one available in the evenings. She persisted and felt that even this professor with all her biases had something to teach her. Sheila felt that as a work in progress, she owed it to herself to see past all the pain and learn.

I don't see myself as a student. I see myself as someone who is trying to be a student. I'm not a complete student. My life won't let me be, because I have those other roles. If I had to rank them on a scale of one to five with one being the lowest, I'd give myself a two as a student. My family would be ranked number five; my job would be number four; my community time, family church, choir practice would be number three; and then school would be number two. Number one would be rest. I will sometimes bend over backwards and let some things go for a while just to make sure that I am getting in enough study time.

I don't socialize that much other than going to church and attending choir practice. I don't talk on the phone to friends anymore or work with community clubs or do volunteer things in the community. It has deeply affected my relationship with my husband. We don't have that much coziness time together. You know how sometimes you just want to snuggle up in bed and watch TV and talk. We don't do that like we used to. I miss that. We do still talk, but we talk about the struggles that I'm having in school and about my school day. But I'm going to make it this time. I guess.

So Sheila's educational efforts occurred in an environment that she found large, overwhelming, and isolating. It was doubly burdensome for Sheila that she had dropped in and out of this same school environment several times. Each time she returned she was dealing with school administrators who knew that she had tried before and had not succeeded. She was determined that she would finish school at her own pace. Another attribute that helped her to survive was her positive attitude about the demands that were placed on her. When she had to stop school for a time, she did it. However, she would not let such circumstances provide an excuse to quit and never try again. Using a part-time approach to course work that is characteristic of reentry women, Sheila made it. She has graduated. She has advanced in her job.

CHAPTER 9

Making a Way: Reflections and Lessons Learned

Introduction

The educational experiences of Black females are notably different than the experiences of other groups. From primary school through higher education, their lives are touched either overtly or covertly by racism and sexism. Since Mary Jane Patterson became the first American Black woman to graduate from college in 1862, the history of Black women's higher education documents that their paths have consistently been one of struggle, confrontation, resistance, negotiation, and marginality. This marginal existence also occurs in the reentry experiences of Black women.

Racism and sexism, the major dividing lines of American society, impact the educational experiences of Black women in many ways. As Blacks, they are thought to be intellectually and morally inferior. As women, they are held to task for the alleged inadequacy of their gender's intellect and a proclivity for subservience, but they are not accorded the benefit of a pedestal and the protection said to be guaranteed the weaker sex. Black women are subordinated by their gender within their racial group and also subjugated because of their race and gender in the larger society. The duality of their position as the conduit of two types of oppression carries into the classroom since education is a reflection of the society that produces it. These issues are brought into the classroom by the socialization process that occurs in the family and other social institutions. The education histories of Black women read differently from those of other disenfranchised groups, such as White females and Black males.

Making Your Own Way

There is much common ground to be found in the triumph and struggles of most reentry women, Black and White alike. Yet the stories of the women in this book mark a ground that is distinct. Despite the hardships found in their accounts, they still found a way to make a way when none seemed apparent.

When they felt like giving up, one of the ways in which the sistahs carried on was by reaching out to other women who were in positions similar to theirs. Reentry women often help each other, especially when they know that one of the members of their rank needs help. Unfortunately, it seems to be a characteristic of this group not to ask for help. But fortunately intuition and generosity are also traits of this population. So that when reentry women share the same classrooms or programs, they find and support each other.

Many colleges and universities have begun to capitalize on this inclination and have formed support groups or arranged activities to unite nontraditional women students. These groups have formed circles of support that offer babysitting services, financial aid, and transportation to members. Occasionally, they have found ways to encourage the administration to recognize their numbers and acknowledge their importance to the college. Some institutions have responded by establishing more flexible hours and scheduling more weekend and evening classes.

Another successful outgrowth of reentry women getting together to talk has been the establishment of mentorships. In some cases, senior students who appear to gravitate toward the more junior students give advice and tips on how to survive the academic environment. In other instances, students form study partnerships or groups, especially to get through science and math courses. Soon they find themselves trading books, forming escort walk patrols for evening students who drive to campus, and trading information on which professors to take and which to avoid.

Obstacles on the Way: Real and Imagined

From my conversations with women who have returned to school, I found three commonalities: fear, doubt, and timidity. In addition, nontraditional women also face institutional barriers that problematize their sojourns. Generally the fear is multifaceted. They fear the new environment, fear that they won't fit in, and fear that they won't finish school. Societal conditioning is the origin of these fears more than any reality the women have experienced. It's quite expected that there would be anxiety about joining a new environment. However, for many of the women who are returning after dropping out years earlier, the setting is not completely foreign. Besides many of these nontraditional women students have faced other new surroundings in the workplace and social settings. Yet, the fear of school on the first day takes them back to a place of childhood vulnerability. One woman said she could hear again all those irrational fears: "Suppose the teacher doesn't like me" or "Suppose no one will play with me." Juanita spoke of thinking that no one was sitting next to her because maybe they thought she didn't belong there or no one liked her.

The fear of not fitting in should be one that is quickly dispelled since so many reentry women now occupy seats in the college classroom. Mature women students compose almost half of the female population in college. But numbers do not equal comfort and this new environment inspires isolationist thinking that says you're different from the others, even the ones who look like you.

Another major apprehension is the fear of not finishing. Rarely does a runner in a race take to the starting line worrying that she won't finish. Yet often reentry women students say that they imagine the "what ifs" that might prevent them from finishing, however unimaginable and irrational. Nevertheless women report being immobilized by this irrational fear during school registration, while sitting in class, and even during graduation ceremonies.

Next to fear, doubt earns a firm place in the everyday lives of women who return to college. In fact they go hand in hand, one supporting the other in a cyclical dance of "I can'ts." Remember Cathy was so afraid that she would not be accepted into her community college's summer enrichment program that when she was turned away because the program had reached capacity, she petitioned the administration until they relented. When she was accepted, she called and decided to withdraw her application because she doubted her ability to accomplish this new goal. She kept saying to herself, "I can't do this," and "What if I'm too old?" or "What if I'm not smart enough?"

Nontraditional college students doubt their abilities and their reasons for entering school. When surrounded by younger students, who are often quicker to answer questions and to take risks, mature women students sometimes feel out of place; they frequently pose questions about whether they are smart enough, quick enough, or possess enough energy. Overwhelmingly the answers are yes. In fact, reentry women students, Black and White, succeed in college and routinely have averages higher than traditional college students. Yes, mature students may appear slower than younger students because as part of the natural process of aging, the mind is required to sort through more data to retrieve an answer. The process can take longer but does not necessarily mean that a student's mind is slower. For instance, Jean related in her narrative that she not only knew the information that was in the text, but knew the facts from living through the experiences. According to her, sometimes the two sources of information were contradictory. As for the abundance of energy possessed by traditional students being an asset not possessed by more mature students, it appears that the experience of the adult student, which brings with it knowledge about pacing yourself, wins out in most circumstances.

The third issue, timidity, dictates many of the behaviors of adult women students. Timidity probably connects with how the women are socialized as girls who should be ladylike and therefore nonassertive and nonconfrontational. Reentry women tend to be people who play nice and put others' needs ahead of their own. In the classroom this translates into not asking for what you need, silencing concerns, failing to volunteer for choice assignments, and waiting for your turn. Such actions are deadly in the Socratic milieu of the college classroom. Not only must students speak out, but in most instances they must contest to be recognized and rewarded for their work. There were many examples in the sistahs' stories of times when they could not speak up or go for the brass ring because they were timid or struggled with feelings of nonentitlement. Beth told how she had to find the courage to finally make her teacher realize that she was not a traditional student and that her adult schedule sometimes unexpectedly intruded into her school life. Her speech teacher had failed Beth because she arrived late to deliver an in-class speech. Beth had been delayed by car problems and explained to her teacher that she didn't just walk across campus from her dorm like most of the traditional students. Expressing this sentiment and addressing the teacher was difficult for Beth. For many returning students, the directness, consumer orientation, and assertiveness of their younger classmates are unsettling.

The final issue mentioned by this group of reentry women were the institutional barriers, such as inconvenient class schedules, remote campus locations, limited registration times, daytime office hours, unsympathetic and misinformed staff and faculty. Although nontraditional women students over the age of twenty-five, who are usually married with children, are flooding back into colleges, institutions have been slow to respond to their needs. Unlike World War II GIs who filled the classrooms of the 1940s and 1950s, these women usually carry the primary responsibilities for childcare and the household. In addition, the majority of the women work part-time or full-time outside of the home without the luxury of a stipend, which was paid to the former servicemen on the GI Bill. Therefore, outside responsibilities and their ability to continue to perform these duties directly affect school participation.

In an attempt to negotiate obstacles that interfere with school attendance, adult women who have returned to school often attend part-time, adjust their courseload relative to their outside demands, and choose colleges in proximity to their homes. Responding to inconvenient registration and college business hours has meant establishing a support network for most reentry women students. The women in this book reported working alternate work schedules to enable them to reserve the time needed to stand in long and unpredictable registration lines or to allow them to go to the campus to buy books, attend special events, visit professors during their daytime office hours, go to the library before class, or pay fees at the college's business offices. For those women who can't get away from work or other responsibilities to accomplish these tasks, students either find school friends, family members, sympathetic college personnel, or someone in their support network to help.

A Way Traversed

"Making a way out of no way" is a saying from my cultural experience that evokes rich images and deep understandings. When I hear it, my mind's eye sees the family who lived up the street from mine when I was a young girl. They were indigent and had twelve children. Somehow they managed to feed, clothe, and educate all of the children. The phrase also reminds me of the times when my parents would be mired in financial despair but steadfastly maintained that some way they would continue to pay for my sister and me to attend Catholic school because the education was superior to that found at the segregated public schools.

When Marcie used this adage in her description, I knew immediately that it aptly described the stories in this book. For in these few words were the circumstances of all the women with whom I spoke. Cathy lived below the poverty line in a housing project and although she had no personal transportation she made it to school everyday. Lynda survived a life that hints of abuse, crippling medical problems, and adult dependent children, to finally insist on her dream of school. Beth and Sheila, both scarred by poverty, found ways to survive and to make life better for their offspring. Marcie, although privileged by birth, has been affected by colorism and family and societal expectations that simultaneously frighten and beckon her to the reentry process. And as the most educationally elite of the respondents, Jean and Faye found their lives defined and possibly constrained by group membership. As Faye implied, alternatives would have opened to her had she been a man or had she been White.

Making a way out of no way means not letting anything stand in your way when you are discouraged. My journey toward reentry began when my Mama Dear reminded me that my reasons for not returning to school were invalid. She told me that my excuses of being too old, too weary, and too poor were inconsequential with the reply, "You're going to be all of those things anyway. You might as well be them with letters behind your name." And so, my rationalizations stripped away, I found a way.

Each of the eight women in this book has persisted in making a way when no way seemed apparent. Too often the choices were made from a menu of few or no choices. And the choices made were accompanied by sacrifices to personal safety and health—Faye's car accident, Cathy's walk to school along a dangerous highway, Marcie's nighttime and early morning train rides to school. And all of this to face a goal that when attained does not guarantee a better future, for there are always the constraints of racism, sexism, classism, and colorism to be factored into the equation. So reentry women returned to school and each in her own way made a way out of no way, with the understanding that she was engaged in a game where the rules, stakes, and conditions were relative to her unique position as a Black woman in a society that values neither her race nor her gender.

Returning to school was an exciting and worthwhile endeavor for each of the women who shared their stories in this book. When asked if they had any regrets, the most frequent reply was that they wished they had gone back earlier or they wished they had never interrupted their schooling. Each found ways to change their lives by going back to school. For Jean, Faye, and Sheila, it meant increases in pay on their existing jobs. School opened new avenues for Cathy, Lynda, and Marcie by providing opportunities for new careers and routes out of poverty or away from parental dependence. As for Beth and Juanita, school opened their eyes to the barriers they had each erected in their own paths.

Indeed school for all of the sistahs, to some degree, removed blinders, broadened horizons, or provided new perspectives. Education for reentry women is potent in its effect. As Jean put it, "You're finally old enough to pay for it, take it seriously, do it right, and savor the doing."

APPENDIX

A Qualitative Analysis of the Academic Experiences of Black Reentry Women

Introduction

Representing over 50 percent of all female college students, adult women who return to college comprise the fastest growing segment of the college population (Evangelauf, 1992; Schmittroth, 1995; Touchton & Davis, 1991). Women have been returning to college in record numbers since the 1970s. Typically, the incursion of these students has been studied with an objective surveillance which noted the homogeneity of the group as mostly female, making it a gendered phenomenon. By definition these women either interrupted their college educations for five or more years, delayed entering college directly after high school, or are over thirty-five years old (Lewis, 1988). They are therefore older than the traditional college pupil. Reentry women can most often be divided into three groups: career women who have returned to school for employment advancement; women who are coping with an empty nest, retirement or widowhood; and first time college women (Pierre, 1989; Rifenbary, 1995).

Within this major academic groundswell are women of all races and ethnicities. However if conclusions are drawn from the literature, it could be assumed that this group is composed of "generic learners" (Johnson-Bailey, 1994) who are White, middle-aged, middle class, and whose concerns and experiences are similar across the group. There are several inherent disadvantages in viewing this group generically. Foremost, it presents an inaccurate view of the group. In addition, such conclusions belie the large numbers of Black females who are included in the catch-all category of reentry students. Another detriment to this myopic perspective is that researchers have begun to make generalizations about reentry women based on the available data (Caffarella & Olson, 1993).

Black women comprise the largest number of students of color at the graduate and undergraduate level (Evangelauf, 1992) and at the reentry level (Johnson-Bailey, 1994). Yet, their numbers are disproportionately low when compared to their representation in the population and retention remains a dilemma for Black women in higher education (Merriam & Caffarella, 1991). Only three studies have been identified in the more than 1,000 published which have included Black women as respondents. Two of these studies, the Demos (1979) and the Kaplan (1982) studies, did not recognize or report any differences between the female respondents by race or even conjecture that differences may exist. In a third study Henry (1985) focused on Black women as a research group and provided a broad profile of the group. Henry (1985), however, did not present an in-depth picture of who these Black women were and of how they were faring in their academic sojourns.

The problem, then, is that Black women as a group go unnoticed and unresearched, and their specific and individual needs remain unaddressed by academia. In light of the absence of Black women in the reentry research, this study was designed to examine the educational narratives of reentry Black women in an effort to determine the ways that the dynamics of the larger society, which often negatively impacts their lives, are played out in higher education. *The purpose of this qualitative research project was to examine the educational narratives of reentry Black women in higher education to determine what common experiences shape their academic tenure.*

Methodological and Theoretical Framework

The theoretical framework for this study was twofold. First, the concept of Black feminist thought with its theories and extensive writings provided guidance and helped establish the parameters for this research (Collins, 1989, 1990; Davis, 1981; Giddings, 1984; hooks, 1984, 1989; Hull, Bell-Scott, & Smith, 1982; Lorde, 1984; Wallace, 1978). This perspective refers to a body of knowledge that expresses the idea that the daily living of Black women in a society that is racist and sexist has produced a collective consciousness that resists being defined as less than, resists being stereotyped as undesirable, and seeks to define and empower its members by interpreting existence as a triumph. Second, using this oppositional world view and its resulting epistemology encourages the researcher to use experience as a criterion for assessing knowledge and to use dialogue as a method of inquiry.

Theoretical Framework

Based on the objective stance with which Black women have been examined in past research studies, assumptions were made about Black women that allowed them to be placed neatly but incorrectly into the universal categories of Blacks and women. Since the researcher on this study was a Black woman, this project was approached with premises that differed from earlier studies. The primary supposition, which was based on an experiential knowledge base, accepted foremost that Black women, in reference to their lives and concerns, stood apart at times from White women and from Black men. A theoretical framework that used this same stance as its conceptual framework was Black feminist thought and its resulting epistemology.

By definition Black feminist thought extends from Black feminism which is a movement that addresses issues of race, gender, class, and color as they pertain to Black women. It is maintained that Black women's lives are negatively impacted by racism and sexism and that as a consequence they are more often members of the working class and the working poor. As a result of this constant awareness of difference, the theoretical writings of Black feminist thought posit that Black women conceptualize their existence as unique and their place as tenuous and uncertain. Therefore, they maintain an oppositional worldview.

Design of the Study

The corollary methodology from such an oppositional agenda necessitates that the researcher be sensitive to the position and history of Black women, that she accept the culture-specific practice of regarding experience as a criterion for assessing knowledge, and that the research process be dialogic. The nature of Black feminist thought requires that the perspective of the researcher be evident. To accomplish this, it is required that the researcher attend to the inherent power dynamics in the research process. In an effort to be congruous with this methodological issue, the personal narrative of the author and her accompanying perspective were made part of the study in two distinct ways. As a prerequisite to the study and in an effort to sensitize the researcher to the difficulty and tension of the interview process, the author was interviewed by a methodological specialist using the same guide that would be used with the respondents. Second, the inclusion of the author's narrative highlighted the commonalities between her story and the stories of her respondents. This overlap indicates the proficiency of the process as a tool for effective data collection. Additionally, the differences between the author's narrative and those of the respondents stand as an analytic litmus test to highlight the integrity of the process.

Using narrative analysis as the specific methodology (Casey, 1993; Etter-Lewis, 1993; Luttrell, 1993), a semistructured interview format, accompanied by an interview guide and an opening statement (see attached), were employed to solicit responses from the subjects. The interview guide and the follow-up questions never addressed the topics of race, gender, class, or color. Instead the respondents were asked open-ended questions (Bogdan & Biklen, 1982) about their most pleasant and unpleasant memories of school and they responded as Witherell and Noddings (1991) had predicted—with stories centered in cultural concerns. These tape-recorded answers were then transcribed and analyzed as text (McAdams, 1988; Ochberg, 1988; Riessman, 1993).

The interviews were reciprocal in nature. As stories were solicited from the participants, they would often in turn ask the researcher to tell them about her academic experiences. The researcher asked questions that allowed the participants the freedom to independently frame their stories. The interview lengths varied, with the briefest being two hours and the most lengthy being four and one-half hours. The interviews departed from traditional interviewee/interviewer format in that they were dialogic in nature. The women seemed more collaborators than respondents: 1) they asked questions; 2) they gave advice; and 3) they occasionally redirected the course of the interview. In addition, in some instances the women and the interviewer worked as the interview progressed, performing household chores, yard work, addressing envelopes, and preparing and eating meals. The interviews were transcribed and emerging themes identified. The methodology used in this study combined biographic techniques (Alexander, 1988; Denzin, 1989; McAdams, 1988; Ochberg, 1988), culturally specific linguistic analysis (Etter-Lewis, 1993), culturally specific analysis (Collins, 1989; Gluck & Patai, 1991; Witherell & Noddings, 1991), ethnographic practices (Casey, 1993), and narrative analysis (Etter-Lewis, 1993; Reissman, 1993).

In narrative analysis every utterance, even repetitions and noises are regarded as part of the data. Speech patterns were noted in the text and also served to reveal aspects of the stories that were not overtly evident in the initial recording (Etter-Lewis, 1993). Quotes were dissected from the original transcript and infused liberally in the written report to support various emerging themes. This procedure assured that the women's voices would be apparent throughout the work. There were two major methodological tools used in analysis. The first was the biographic tenets set forth by Denzin (1989).

The second most often used technique of analysis applied to the data was Alexander's nine identifiers of salience (1988): primacy, omission, frequency, emphasis, negation, isolation, incompletion, uniqueness, and errors.

The Sample

The purposeful sample, which included the author, consisted of three graduate and five undergraduate women between the ages of thirty-four and fifty-four. The colleges designated for this sampling were 1) a predominately Black women's college; 2) a predominately White women's college; 3) a large southern state university's main campus; 4) a two-year community college; and 5) a religious affiliated four-year university. To attend to the cultural diversity of available settings, the participants were selected from varied collegiate backgrounds in terms of the racial and gender composition of the student body, size, and type of institution. The sample was obtained by contacting college reentry programs, identifying a pool of potential respondents, and then screening them using specific criteria to achieve an ample array of participant backgrounds.

The definition of reentry students that characterized them as women over thirty was utilized with the expressed belief that women in this age category would provide a reflective aspect to their interviews (Gilligan, 1982). The women were asked to choose a pseudonym and if they opted not to select a name they were given a fictitious one. Only one participant chose a pseudonym, Marcie. The others were assigned names by the researcher.

The demographic profiles of the eight women, Sheila, Marcie, Faye, Lynda, Cathy, Beth, Jean, and Juanita (the author of this Appendix) included age, marital status, school history, reentry experience, number of children, and class origins (see chart). Analysis revealed that most of the women attended segregated elementary schools and integrated high schools.

And the "Way" Was Difficult

Black women as a group have experiences in the United States that make their lives different. They are simultaneously affected by gender and race issues. Their embodiment of both concerns distinguish them from the larger groups in which they are always subsumed in the literature and in statistics, Blacks and women. The life experiences of Black women are distinctly different from those of White women and Black men.

The experiences of Black women in the world are different from those of other groups because of the established societal hierarchies of race and gender (Collins, 1990; Giddings, 1984; hooks, 1984; 1989; Hull, Scott, & Smith,

Demographic Background and School History of Respondents

NAME	AGE	MARITAL STATUS	SCHOOL HISTORY	REENTRY EXPERIENCE	NUMBER OF CHILDREN	CLASS ORIGINS
Sheila	38	M	segregated K - 8	4 yr White university	2/ ages 2 & 13	Rural Poor
Marcie	34	S	integrated K - 12	4 yr. Women's HBCU	none	Upper Middle
Lynda	54	WI	segregated K - 12	2 yr. White college	4 adult	Working Class
Cathy	36	D	segregated K - 8 integrated HS	2 yr. White college	2/ ages 5 & 11	Urban Poor
Beth	38	M	segregated K - 8 integrated HS	4 yr. White women's college	6/ ages 16 & 17 4 adult	Rural Poor
Jean	53	WI	segregated K - 12 HBCU undergrad	graduated 4 yr. White university	2 adult	Middle Class
Faye	43	M	segregated K - 8 integrated HS HBCU undergrad	graduated 4 yr. White university	None	Middle Class
Juanita	40	M	segregated K - 8 integrated HS White university undergrad	graduated 4 yr. White university	1/ age 17	Working Class

Key: Abbreviations

M   -   married
S   -   single
D   -   divorced
WI   -   widowed
W   -   predominantly White
HBCU   -   historically Black college or university

1982; Wallace, 1978). Racism and sexism as societal forces harshly impact the lives of Black women (Amott & Matthaei, 1991; Hacker, 1992) and are evidenced in their economic standing, high mortality rate, and low rate of educational attainment. Therefore, class also becomes inextricably linked to the lives of Black women. Black women and their children stand apart as the poorest of the poor in America. Since the position of this group in a hierarchal society that trades on race, gender, and class privileges is severely impacted, then, certainly their experiences in academia as reentry women should not be assumed to be addressed by studies that do not locate them as the central focus.

Black women have neither their race, gender, nor class status on which to trade in a world that grants entitlements based on each. These issues which encompass the lives of Black women in this American culture are complex and interlock in all areas of their lives. The place of Black women in the general population translates into an inability to acquire power and privilege. Existing with this knowledge of a presumed lesser position in society has produced an internalized form of self-hatred and intraracial discrimination that especially affects Black women (Russell, Wilson, & Hall, 1992). Since academia does not exist in a vacuum, it is only logical to assume that the same forces and issues that are present in society in general are ever present within the classroom.

So it is imperative that when the lives of Black women in college are studied that the concerns of race, gender, and class discrimination be addressed. The importance of examining the educational circumstances of Black women becomes quite clear particularly when in the last twenty years American colleges have experienced a dramatic influx of nontraditional students many of whom have been Black women.

In an effort to capture the experiences in their own words, the participants were asked to give a simile or metaphor for their reentry process. Marcie, a thirty-four-year old who was attending a historically Black college or university (HBCU), struggled at first, but then she said:

> If you don't bend with the situation that you find yourself in, you're gonna break. 'Cause who am I? I'm a Black woman in America and that's as handicapped as you can get. You know? And I can't remember what comedian said it, but it's the truth. And what this is, is trying to make a way out of no way. That's it! I don't have a pot to piss in and a window to throw it out of, but I want it. And this is how I have to go about getting. I need the paper [college diploma].

Her statement capsulized the experiences of the other women and gave a title to the dissertation on which this study is based, "Making a Way Out of

No Way." Other answers to this question of providing a simile or metaphor to describe the schooling experience were just as telling. Cathy, a thirty-six-year-old community college student, characterized it as a roller coaster ride that often made her physically ill and Juanita, a forty-year-old doctoral student, portrayed it as "skipping barefoot through broken glass; on some days you hit bigger pieces of glass than you did on others."

For each of the women in this study the act of returning to school was one of individual bravery. For some it meant defying the norm of what others in their social circle were doing and for others it meant inconvenience and an interruption of their family and personal schedules. Five of the women in the study had full-time careers while they attended college, explaining that they kept their jobs either because they needed them or that good jobs were hard to find especially for Black women. The women were equally divided between part-time and full-time school attendance.

For each woman returning to school was part of a directive to do better than their mothers. All were seeking better lives, some for themselves and others for their children. Each considered education a necessary foundation for survival. They approached school with a history of previous marginality. For most of the women early schooling was separate and unequal from the experiences of their White cohort. For all of them it had involved lessons of survival. Even in all-Black settings there seemed to be challenges. Yet, they all approached reentry, as Marcie said, "to make a way out of no way." This old adage from the Black community depicts struggle against formidable odds. It refers to surviving a trial that you were not expected to survive and one that it was hoped you could not endure. The reasons and accounts of why the women returned to school are individual profiles of persistence and survival. Yet there were commonalities in their motivations.

All of the women approached school with a cognizance of marginality. In their separate interviews they defined in various ways a knowledge of being Black in America, a position that DuBois (1903/1953) calls double-consciousness and Collins (1990) refers to as an outsider/insider perspective. Yet, they did not predispose themselves toward the negative any more in school than they would have in society in general. In response to the question, "How would you describe your overall school experience?" Faye described the environment as "hostile until all the flags are raised and everyone knows where everyone stands." She further characterized academia for Blacks in this manner: "Well, until there was a chance to demonstrate ability, I just think that a question mark registers subconsciously in Black/White relationships."

Such statements as the ones made by Faye evidence that the women did not see school as a separate environment apart from the rest of the world. Indeed school does not occur apart from the real world. It occurs in the midst of society and so the episodes in these women's schooling experiences were, according to them, a microcosm of familiarity.

Roadblocks Along the Way

At first glance, reentry seemed an easier process for the graduate women. All three had attended undergraduate school directly after high school and had the success of a bachelor's degree behind them. Yet, reentering meant balancing a full-time job, a family, and school for each woman. None of the women considered quitting their jobs as an option and none considered going to school part-time. Jean felt that she could endure anything for a year or two. Graduate school for Jean meant a drive across town three nights a week and extra classes for the summers. For Faye and Juanita it meant, respectively, a weekly six-hundred mile commute and a weekly one-thousand mile commute. In retrospect Faye said it was never a matter of "Will I?" but a matter of "How will I?"

For the undergraduate women the reentry process was also a series of trying circumstances that involved long work and school hours. Like the graduate women, quitting work was not a choice open to Sheila. She is the only undergraduate woman of the five who worked full-time while pursuing a degree. It was a chance encounter with a friend that encouraged Sheila to try college a third time. This time she was wiser and older, and her husband, a recovering alcoholic, had been sober for two years. She finally began to believe that she could complete her degree and support from a co-worker was all she needed to make the decision to return to school:

> I said, "Oh no school is not for me. I can't go back to school. I don't know. Uh huh." I said, "I'm just as content as I am. I'm just going to continue to do what I'm doing." She kept saying, "Go back to school and I'll come to your graduation." And just the thought of hearing the word graduation. It was like motivation.

Similarly, for Beth it was encouragement from another person that spurred her into the reentry process. Beth had just moved to a new town and a chance meeting with a new minister led her to the church affiliated women's college she now attends. College was not talked of much in her family of origin but during her second marriage to a college-educated man, she felt a need to get a college degree. So she took advantage of the opportunity to go to college when it was presented. In the beginning she thought of quitting several times, but she now says that to get her to leave they would have to "lock the doors."

The determination exhibited by Cathy is just as admirable. She doesn't have a car but manages to make school every day. She said that once she started school she could not stop. It was starting that took courage, recounting a private debate she waged:

> I was afraid. The fear of failure. It's been too long. I won't fit. And so. And when I finally made the decision to go I think it was the best decision I could have made because I was staying home. I was on the system. I'm still on the system. But, ah, I was feeling a little low self-esteem because I didn't want to go back to slinging hamburgers. And so I said, "Well let me see how I can utilize—since I'm already on the system. Let me see how the system can help me. And so I can get off the system."

She was initially rejected by the community college to which she had applied because the program was full. After many pleas from Cathy, the school created an extra space in the program. She has been enrolled ever since.

Juanita's story is analogous to Cathy's. It began with excuses of why she could not and it also began with rejection. Her mother and husband support team eliminated her excuses one by one. When she finally applied to college her application was rejected because they said her undergraduate grade point average did not demonstrate the ability to handle graduate school. She was devastated. Her GPA was a 3.5 and she had finished college in three years by taking an overload of courses. When a friend shared a similar horror story that involved the same university, she found the courage to appeal and was granted an unconditional acceptance. In spite of this she knew her reentry process would be an uphill battle.

Similarly, Marcie's road to reentry has not been an uncomplicated route. She has been in college longer than any of the other women. After completing four years as a traditional undergraduate, she left college without a degree. A series of jobs netted her a bleak future. Like the other undergraduate women, Marcie feels that a college degree is her passage to a better life. She reapplied to the women's college she had previously attended. As an explanation of her earlier unsuccessful tenure, she said, "I was young. I was dumb. I want you to look at me again." They did.

Unlike many of the other women in this study, Marcie has not been able to be a full-time student. She has been a reentry student on and off since 1985. Sometimes she did not have a car or the tuition money. Determined to do it alone, she will not ask her parents for help. Despite trying circumstances, outwardly she appears optimistic. She explains her outlook and her unrelenting educational endeavor:

> Like I'm not happy. Ya'll make me sound like Rebecca of Sunny Brook Farm. You know I'm not. But I think there is humor in almost every situation. You know I said and what you have to remember before you start laughing or

crying or ranting or raving, reacting to whatever is going on around you is, is it worth all that? And is it alright? Are you here? Cause my logic is, if I woke up I'm suppose to be here today. Which means whatever comes, I'm suppose to be able to handle in some type of way [laughs]. . . . Ah, if you don't bend with the situation that you find yourself in, you're gonna break. Cause who am I? I'm a Black woman in America and that's as handicapped as you can get. You know? And I can't remember what comedian said it, but it's the truth. And what this is—is trying to make a way out of no way. That's it. I don't have a pot to piss in and window to throw it out of but I want it. And this is how I have to go about getting. I need the paper.

Race

A review of the literature regarding Black college women (Cuthbert, 1942/ 1987; Fleming, 1984; Noble, 1956; Player, 1948/1987) reveals that race and racism are prominent themes in higher education. This evaluation held true in the educational narratives of the women studied. As illustrated by the opening interview statement and interview guide (see attached), race was not an issue or a question about which the women were questioned. Yet, each woman advanced the matter of race, not only to describe her life, but also to talk about racism in her education history. Race was initially discussed by many of the women as they recalled the circumstances of their early education or their early lives.

The accounts were divided between classroom incidents and social interactions. Several of the stories related by the women were seen by the women as overtly racist. Sheila, a thirty-eight-year-old full-time student at a White research university, discussed a psychology professor who would tell embarrassing stories about Blacks and then challenge her Black students with, "Now if I'm wrong about ya'll, speak up and defend yourselves." Sheila recalled one story that the instructor told about her Black cleaning lady who had gone from job to job and who could not hold a job because of her poor performance. According to the professor, the woman was failing at her new job and expected to be fired once again. Instead the professor recalled that she made the woman do the task over and over until she got it right. Her point was that you have to treat some groups like children to make them accountable or else they "will never succeed at anything." Sheila felt humiliated and recalled that she and the other Black students in the class would exchange uncomfortable glances on the occasions when such racist stories were told.

A similar classroom scene was related by Cathy who had an English teacher who showed several films that depicted distorted pictures of life in the rural South where the Black characters were presented as lazy, ignorant, and inferior:

The films that she would present to the class would use certain terms like [racial epithets for Blacks] . . . I was the only African American in class . . . I don't know if she did that to incite discussion. But it never came up. No one mentioned it. I was afraid . . .

Not all of the incidents told by the women were so blatantly racist. Others mentioned feeling ignored by teachers when they raised their hands or being treated in what they perceived as an unfair way. Faye, a forty-year-old graduate student, gave an example that typified the classroom incidents described by the women:

Usually in what I've observed, when Whites challenge the information, they'll [the teachers] say something to the effect, "Well there could be later research on that information. I would be interested in knowing more about it. Can you locate that?" But I've had [the same] professors become defensive when I tried the same thing. It's like, "You don't know more than I know. This is a fact."

She explained, "You already know that the rules may not be the same . . . just because of the pigmentation of your skin. But I've long since past worrying about what I can not change."

Jean, a fifty-three-year-old graduate student, recalls an incident in which the rules were arbitrarily applied to her. She had asked to go to another room to take an exam. The professor had just allowed another student to do this. He adamantly refused to let her go and offered no explanation. She felt that something in his manner let her know that he didn't trust her. Jean later conjectured that the scenario might not have been racial, but that it felt analogous to other racist incidents that had occurred in her life.

The women also discussed the social interactions that usually result from classroom relationships as a problem area for them. Several recalled being excluded from study groups, having their contributions stifled during small group activities, and not being invited to after-class dinners and coffee get-togethers. While they knew that with traditional college students the awkward age differences accounted for some of the exclusion, they felt that with other reentry students there was no excuse other than racism. Beth recalled asking everyone in the class about forming a study group and being told by other students that they were not interested. One day while studying in the library Beth ran into a study group from her class. She explained that it was not necessarily "intentional racism." People are just "more comfortable within their own little groups." But she added that the result was the same: she studies and struggles in isolation.

Gender

Gender, while not advanced by the women in this study as a restraint to their lives or educational endeavors, was observed to be a factor that consistently affected their lives and the way in which they approached their educations. This was most apparent around the issues of self-doubt, child care, household responsibilities, and relationships.

Self-doubt, a common element with all of the participants, was cited as a particularly gendered phenomenon among women students (Sadker & Sadker, 1994). It is especially common among reentry women (Pitts, 1992; Safman, 1988). The women in this study constantly referred to themselves as not being "as good as other students," or "not good enough to make it." In a tearful moment Lynda, a fifty-four-year-old community college student, told an extreme story of self-doubt that spanned twenty years. She originally registered for school in 1976, but failed to show up for the first day of class. She explained that she just didn't think she'd be able to make it in school and that her husband did not think that it was a good idea either. It would not be until 1996, twenty years later, that she would garner the "courage" to register again and this time attend classes. The second enrollment occurred after her marriage ended.

Child care and household responsibilities were other gender concerns in the stories of the eight women studied. Six of the women in the study were married and/or had children. For these women, their responsibilities did not change when they entered school. The families expected them to continue their old routines of cooking, cleaning, laundry, and car pooling in addition to the new routine of attending school and studying. Beth, whose spouse was also in school, said that the children seemed to respect that he has less time for them and that he needed his study time. However, she said that they were not pleased with the new demands on her time and "They want me to stop and run them all over town as if I don't have homework and as if I am not tired from school."

According to the women, spouses, significant others, and friends did not like that school had cut into their social times. Sheila said that socializing, especially with friends, is a thing of the past:

> I don't socialize that much other than going to church and attending choir practice. I did talk on the telephone to friends, but I don't anymore. I used to be in community clubs, voluntarily do things with the kids in the community, but I can't anymore.

She also explained that her spouse resents the time that she spends studying and discourages her away from it.

Jean, who was unexpectedly widowed at fifty, explained that when her husband was alive she tried to guarantee that school would not interfere:

> I would go to bed with my husband at 11 o'clock. I would set the alarm clock for 3:00 or 4:00 a.m. I'd get up and do my studying then. That way I could still have our family time, so to speak, and have study time too.

However, her husband who had previously completed his master's made no such allowances. In fact Jean helped him with his studies by typing and proof-reading.

Class

More Black women and their children exist below and slightly above the poverty level than any other segment of our society (Hacker, 1992). As a result, class is inextricably tied to the situations of Black women and their families. As the women in this study spoke of their lives, matters of class became apparent, although they were not described by the women as being about "class." Moreover, in Black communities class is often associated with one's education as well as one's economic fortunes (Frazier, 1962). Of the eight women in this study only Marcie's parents were college educated, but Jean's and Faye's fathers had attended school beyond high school. Jean's father was both a licensed contractor and an undertaker. Faye's father had attended the seminary and was accepted in the community as a leader, someone who was well read.

In general, the lives of most of the women were affected by class, if not directly, then indirectly. Considering that all of them, excluding Marcie, grew up in southern states where segregation was the law of the land, they each experienced circumstances, especially in school, that were less than equal to Whites and others who were economically privileged (Weinberg, 1977). Although Jean's father was the school board president and the local mortician, he was the president of the Black school district and the mortician to Black clients only. Faye's father was a Baptist minister but his line of authority and influence was confined to Black Baptist churches and the Black community. Even Marcie recalled that her father was initially drafted into the segregated Army. After his first tenure, he attended college and reenlisted into the integrated Army. And so class boundaries like gender restrictions seemed undeniably connected to the lives of the eight Black reentry women in this study.

Only two of the eight participants in this study are economically disadvantaged. Lynda lives in a rent controlled apartment complex that is socially one step removed from a housing project. Another respondent, Cathy, lives in a housing project with her two children, a five-year-old girl and an eleven-year-old boy. She receives public assistance. She attends school through a government grant from the Department of Family and Children Services. Her financial conditions often intrude on her college aspirations as was the case during the first week of her new school life:

> I will never forget. I remember one morning I left home. I had missed the bus 'cause the bus would come so early in the morning. I had to get up—the children and everything. I just missed the bus. I was determined to get out there. And my class was like at 10:00 and I mistimed it. I didn't time it right. And I thought. I had been driving, but my car wouldn't crank up. I missed my bus. So I decided to walk. I said from where I live to the college is no problem until I started walking. And it was raining and my foot fell in some water. And I looked back I could see my house. And I looked the other way and I couldn't see the college. But I was determined to go. I had to go. I was walking up E____, slish, slosh, slish, slosh. I didn't want to miss, not just cause I had to walk. I wasn't sick. The children weren't sick, and I didn't want to miss it. I was determined to get there.

Cathy's determination has served her well. She has not been able to repair her car and now catches the bus to school every morning. She walks her children to their schools and then walks the one half mile to the bus stop. According to her, the nursing degree is her way out of her present life circumstances.

Marcie, who comes from a privileged family of origin, developed an early assessment of and dislike for class disparities that has followed her into adulthood. Marcie presently works at a local housing project where she leads a girl scout troop for underprivileged children. Even though she lives an upper middle class existence in her parents' home, she considers herself separate from the other students at the prestigious women's college she attends. She explained that not only does her advanced age separate her from the other students, but that their class consciousness and elitist ways are also a boundary between them. Since she will not accept financial help from her parents, she struggles each quarter to pay her tuition, buy books, and seek out sundry part-time jobs that will accommodate her ever-changing school schedule. According to Marcie, her classmates don't understand struggle and have no idea of the kind of despair that affects the lives of many poor women: where is the next meal coming from, do I pay the bills or do I pay tuition, can I afford to buy the optional texts and the study guide?

Familiar "Ways" Revisited

After the themes of racism, sexism, and classism emerged as points in the women's reentry experiences, the women's ways of coping with these issues were examined. In response to the difficult moments in the women's re-entry schooling experiences the women used several coping mechanisms: silence, negotiation, and resistance. These were not new strategies. Over the course of living the women had used these mechanisms to survive and/or to succeed.

Silence

All of the women studied sometimes held their tongues as a way of getting by. At other times they silenced their minds refusing to think so as to avoid the pain. Faye said that, historically, Blacks and women have been conditioned not to ask questions as a way of surviving. Many of the women spoke of silence as a familiar strategy from their familial backgrounds. Cathy and Lynda recalled seeing their mothers go silently to the back of the bus to comply with a segregated system that they privately abhorred.

Silence as a coping mechanism occurred as an internal and external strategy. There were times when a respondent would not think of or face an issue because it was too painful. In such an example, the silence was internal. In other examples the women would refuse to answer questions or participate in activities because they equated silence as the safer course of action. As a strategy silence was particularly surprising given the outspoken nature of the majority of the women. Even the women who expressed no issues of self-doubt used silence as a classroom tactic.

Jean raised the issue of silence in reference to an awkward moment in a Georgia history class. Laughingly she related:

> And in Georgia history class there comes a time when we must deal with Civil Rights and prejudices and Black/White relationships and all of this. . . . I was the only Black in the class—antiquated and Black in the class—which meant that I have had the opportunity to not only read the changes but I've lived the changes. There were times in the class when even the professor felt uncomfortable.

Cathy also found herself in a similar dilemma in which she felt humiliated. She still questions why despite her anger, she never said a word when the teacher showed a series of films that depicted Blacks as lazy, ignorant, and inferior.

> And I never brought it up. I feel that for ah some reason ah that I should have spoken up. . . . But I don't know if I felt that if I had mentioned anything that ah, you know, that it may have affected my grade . . . Because I had to make an A or B you know for the class, in honors. So, I didn't. I was afraid to throw stones when no one else brought it up.

Data Display/Tentative Findings

Categories	Properties/ Subcategories
I. Silence	a. Internal dimensions
	b. External dimensions
II. Resistance	Interaction with others
III. Negotiation	a. Internal
	b. External
	1. teachers
	2. classmates

In response to her feelings, she summoned a long standing coping mechanism, silence. She had learned silence at an early age as the result of a traumatic experience that occurred shortly after the school system was integrated. It seems Cathy asked a question in class that disturbed her new White teacher. Rather than responding to Cathy's question, the teacher glared at her as if "I was asking a dumb question." The class laughed. It was her first experience with a White teacher and White students. She never asked another question during class.

Faye looked at the issue of silence systematically, "Black folk don't ask questions. The children don't ask questions. . . . I think historically we've been encouraged to be quiet, shut up, and it might work out alright." Beth agreed, saying that it was one of the first lessons she learned from her mother:

> She was the kind of person who did teach us, ah, that there could be differences. You know we discussed a lot of things at home. So, she made us aware of, hey this was gonna happen to you. You know, you gotta understand that it's not the person, it's just the way society is cut out. I mean, and that's just you know it was just a fact of life that we had to learn very young. . . . You've got to learn to shut your mouth [laughs] to survive.

Negotiation

The second tactic to emerge was negotiation. This coping strategy occurred both internally and externally in the women's narratives. In several instances the women recounted times when they delayed reacting to situations that involved professors or students. They said that they "thought long and hard" about the best course to pursue, searching for the middle ground or path of least resistance. On other occasions the women negotiated household chores or family responsibilities in order to have time for school. According to Jean, negotiation is a way of life for any minority: Blacks, women, gay men, lesbians, or other people of color. She stated that on a daily basis these groups must weigh options that members of the majority don't have to entertain.

Marcie, Cathy, Jean, and Faye shared that in class they must reach out to students to know where they can find acceptance. Faye says of graduate school, "There are no babies on the beach." She stated that she lives with the knowledge that things are not fair. However, she adds that regardless of this knowledge she still negotiates with fellow students to find acceptance. Faye explained that quite often as a method of negotiation she offers to do the hard job so that she can find acceptance into a group of students. Jean supports this viewpoint: " . . . there's always a little circle that you find yourself being able to be a part of . . . it's not fair, it's uncomfortable, but it's life." Marcie is explicit in her articulation of the negotiation process:

> There's an automatic pilot that I think all Blacks have that deals with survival—on survival mode at all times [laughs]. And it's automatic, you don't turn it on. You don't turn it off. It's automatic. You start looking to see who's nice, who makes eye contact, who's receptive, you know, who doesn't shy away from you in the lunch line, who steps up to you and asks you about homework and says I had problems with number six. Ah, it—that's just the way it is.

Negotiation as a strategy is used in the classroom as well as in the women's personal relationships, especially around family duties and study times for those women who carried the bulk of the prescribed household duties while attending school. There was often bargaining in exchange for the freedom to attend school. Sheila's story exemplifies this negotiation:

> Sometimes I try to study and when I study I'm in bed at 2:00 or 3:00 in the morning. I feel uncomfortable sometimes in my bedroom, but that's where my husband goes to sleep. So we argue, "Turn the light off. How long are you going to study?" I don't feel comfortable leaving home to study, but I wish I could. But I want to be with the family when I study. But I can't study efficiently, properly doing that. For right now it's kind of a struggle. It's very hard trying to find an appropriate place to study. . . . He doesn't understand what it takes because on that part he is not too accepting . . . if I'm not up to it I can't study like I want to late at night. But if I have to, I stay up until 4:00 and then go to work at 8:00 in the morning dragging.

The seemingly impossible negotiation that Sheila has extracted from her life was to relinquish her rest in exchange for some semblance of her previous family life.

Juanita's personal negotiation around the issue of study time was not with her family or husband but with herself. She felt that as a Black women it was impossible for her to walk away from a mid-level management job given that few Black women have such opportunities. So her only choice was:

> I'm up at 6:00 and I get to work around 8:00. Ah, I do my job and leave work about 3 o'clock to come to school. I have to work through my lunch break so that I can leave early ... Ah, I drive about a hundred miles to school. I'm in class from 4:30 to 8:30. Ah, I drive home. A lot of nights I stay up late to study. You know if I have a paper, a particular paper, I see the sun come up in the morning ... Ah, I don't get a lot of sleep. I sleep on weekends. I mean I'm dead on weekends.

Staying up all night became a routine for her that eventually affected her health.

In some small way, all the women juggled demands of work, or children, or husbands and showed an inability to step out of the super Black woman role, where they take care of the world but not themselves (Wallace, 1978). The tendency to sacrifice too much in an attempt to satisfy all demands was not a demonstration of strength or survival but what Scott (1991) referred to as an unhealthy "habit of surviving." A habit that became a routine for all of these reentry women. In sum, negotiation, like silence, appeared an old companion to the eight women studied. It had consistently become a strategy used to balance the powerful dynamics of race, gender, and class. Negotiation was the most frequently used of the three coping strategies and, indeed, was exhibited in many instances before they reentered school.

As a coping mechanism, negotiation was apparent on many levels. The participants negotiated flexible work schedules, negotiated assignments with other students—taking turns doing library work and copying, negotiated transcribing lectures, and negotiated personal responsibilities such as child care and cooking with their partners in an effort to carve out study time.

Resistance

A third tactic in the narratives was resistance. Unlike the other two coping mechanisms, resistance only existed on the external level. It was open defiance of rules or actions that the women perceived as unfair. It was the least used of the coping strategies, but its use seemed more firmly etched in the women's memories. Each of the examples given around the women's stories of resistance were epiphanies (Denzin, 1989) that the women presented as dramatic or pivotal times in their higher education careers. Unlike silence and negotiation, resistance did not appear in all the narratives. On rare occasions when they could not negotiate their way out of a situation and they could not accept silence as an alternative, the women used resistance. The majority of the incidents that involved resistance occurred either in the classroom or with college administrators, involving registration or financial aid. They involved moments when the participants spoke out against what they perceived as attempts to stereotype or silence them.

Resistance routinely involved the simple act of speaking out. These women had been socialized by their families and by society at large to be silent or to negotiate. When the women in this study chose confrontation or resistance, it was an alternative preceded by much thought and internal strife. A common bond shared by seven of the examples of resistance is that they involved a White male as the protagonist. The women seemed to cast White males as the ultimate authority figure. And, therefore, speaking out against them seemed to require maximum effort and courage. Only one woman, Sheila, told of a story that concerned an White female professor.

Jean's stories of resistance were more telling and direct. On one occasion Jean rushed headlong into the conflict. It occurred when a teacher asked his class to explain the new experience of teaching children of another race. She recalled that she fought her urge to set the record straight for what seemed like an eternity of class silence. The class stayed quiet and it seemed to Jean that the question would go unanswered. She had to challenge his worldview because he completely negated the experience of her entire heritage. She recalls,

> I raised my hand and said, What do you mean when all of a sudden you are teaching children of a different race? We [Black women] have been teaching children of a different race all of our lives even though we were the ones with the limited education. We taught them what the bathroom was for and what to do when they went in there and what the spoon and fork was for and where to place them after they picked them up off the table. . . . We taught them all the time . . . So we did not all of a sudden start teaching children of a different race. We taught them all the time. But once they got up large enough to open their mouths and say that "word" we had to start saying, "Yes Ma'am" and "Yes Sir" to them.

Jean recalled that people cleared their throats and shifted uncomfortably in their seats. In this instance Jean chose to resist her White male professor in an effort to acknowledge what was the experience of her "women folk." She explained why she spoke up "I couldn't help myself . . . I could not let the teacher fail to recognize the history of the women folk who came before me. I was also old enough to remember. I was old enough to know better."

Beth recalled resisting a Women's Studies teacher's definition of women that did not include the experiences of Black women. In a similar incident, Juanita found that she needed to speak out to defend her research:

In the middle of a mock dissertation defense one of the students said to the professor that she hoped I would have Whites on my committee because my dissertation topic, which centered on Black women, seemed racist. On my behalf, a Black student in the corner advised that the student making the statement should make sure that she had Blacks on her committee to avoid the same. Before I knew it I could not hold it in any longer. My work had been criticized often as irrelevant since it was only about Black women. I told the class that just because my work was about Black women did not make it racist or unimportant. However, since their work excluded Blacks and all minority by design of the sample, but made claims of universality, they needed to check their own racist intentions.

More acts of resistance occurred with the participants and school administrators than with the women in this study and their professors. One participant, Marcie explained that she only interacted with administrators when it was absolutely necessary, such as registration and fee payment. Cathy's story of a registration conflict typifies the experiences of the group. It happened during what should have been a pleasant experience. Cathy was attempting to register for an honors English class. She explained that at her community college this was a rarity for Blacks. According to her, a student must either score very high on the Standard Achievement Test or be recommended by a professor:

I was in line. I was the only Black . . . This administrator who was supervising the line came to me and said . . . "If anyone in the line does not have a letter of invitation or has not been invited into the honors program, they should move to the other line. Well I didn't move because I had a letter. But it was obvious what was happening . . . I watched as the line moved. He didn't ask any of the Whites . . . I was paying close attention. He then asked me, "Were you invited? Do you have a letter from a faculty member?" I was happy to pull it out for him, but at that time for some strange reason he became disinterested. I forced him to look. I put the letter on top of his papers. And I said, "See this is my name . . . I have I.D." It just really ticked me off.

According to Cathy, it was such a distinction to be in the program that she was nervous because she felt she was representing "the race." To those feelings of pressure, she now added the fact that she felt unwanted.

Discussion

The experiences of Black reentry women are largely in direct contrast to the profile of the White middle-aged middle class woman presented in the literature as the typical reentry student. An analysis of their narratives showed that they perceived their position in academia to be different and separate from that of White women and from Black men. In depicting an academic hierarchy in which power and place are considered, the women saw themselves as being at the bottom of the hierarchy. Although it has been suggested that many reentry women return to school in response to the empty nest syndrome, as displaced homemakers seeking marketable training, or as career women seeking further advancement (Pierre, 1989), these subjects were unique in that they did not fit into any of those categories. In addition, none of the women in this study returned to school with the ideation of self-actualization which is also discussed in the literature as a reason for reentry. All the women stated that they were returning to school in hopes of gaining access to a better life and certainly a better job, but clarified their answers by suggesting that they realized that school advancement was not a guarantee to career advancement. They merely hoped an advanced degree would help them with their careers, but allowed that they were pessimistic because they did not perceive the world as being fair to Black women. As one of the women put it, "We [Black women] must be 105 percent qualified in order to succeed." In their explanations was an understanding that their race and gender would remain a lurking variable in determining their lives.

While most research on reentry women states that variables such as marriage, children, past successful school participation, and family background are strong indicators of future school enrollment (Anderson & Darkenwald, 1979; Carp, Peterson & Roelfs, 1974; Cross, 1981; Johnstone & Rivera, 1965; Teachman & Paasch, 1989), this was not seen to be true of the women in this study. If the traditional indicators set forth by the literature were applied to the group studied, none of them would have been reentry students. The participants had decided to enter higher education regardless of past school failures and a lack of family support. In addition, seven of the eight women were first generation college students, and did not have a family background that strongly indicated a collegiate path.

Although the women in this study experienced some of the same situational and psychological barriers that have been described as endemic for reentry women, such as doubts about performance, scheduling conflicts, and lack of financial aid (Beer, 1989; Harrington, 1993; Tittle & Denker, 1980), they considered these issues extraneous to other barriers encountered. Therefore, their classification or acknowledgment of such issues as dilemmas, barriers, or traumas was dissimilar because they perceived them differently and ranked them differently in relation to their hierarchy of concerns.

Although the interview guide used to collect the data never addressed the issues of race, gender, class, or color, these subjects emerged as themes in the narratives of each respondent. As maintained by Witherell and Noddings

REENTRY OF BLACK WOMEN

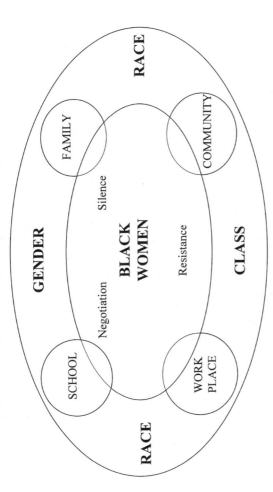

The placement of the women's lives relative to these forces inside and outside of higher education are displayed in this diagram, a graphic representation used to conceptualize the women's lives as a process. The issues of race, gender, and class are depicted in the background surrounding the circle to indicate powerful forces which are ever-present in society. The center circle overlaps the smaller circles which represent the different segments of society: school, workplace, community, and family. The obstacles they encountered in school were no different from those experienced in the other three areas. To cope with old dilemmas, the women relied on familiar strategies (silence, negotiation, and resistance) they had used throughout their lives, to respond to the direct impact of racism, sexism, classism, and colorism in these four social sites.

Source: Johnson-Bailey, J. (1994). Making a way out of no way: An analysis of the education narratives of reentry Black women with emphasis on issues of race, gender, class, and color. Unpublished doctoral dissertation The University of Georgia, Athens.

(1991), culture will always be apparent when subjects are allowed to frame their own stories. And consequently, the women in this study set forth that their lives inside academia mirrored their existences outside the academy. They perceived an enduring hierarchy that paralleled the power and privilege of the secular world. There were assigned roles and rules that served to authorize and to restrain them based on status and place. These rules could be blatantly apparent in student interactions, such as small group activities and networking, or they could be masked within the hidden curriculum. In addition, the practice of exclusion and stereotyping was customary for students and faculty alike because it was so routinely a part of the larger society. Indeed participation in the societal hierarchial subterfuge seemed unconscious and automatic regardless of the expressed intent of the participants.

The strongest deterrent to these women's participation in any schooling process was their classroom and societal encounters that involved racism and sexism. Of primary concern to the group of women in this study were the problems faced in the classroom when they felt excluded, devalued, isolated, and were viewed as less capable. In analysis, the reality of racism and sexism was principal in their consideration of their reentry experience. Similar to their reentry counterparts, the women studied struggled with issues of doubt regardless of their successes (Hall & Sandler, 1982). In this area also they were distinct in that even when they were aware that unfairness might be involved they continued to place themselves in a cycle of self-doubt and discrimination (Luttrell, 1993) and still held themselves accountable for any failures.

All of the women possessed an understanding of the forces that shaped and determined their existences and therefore used an oppositional world view to frame their stories. Using what Dubois (1903/1953) called "double consciousness" and what Collins (1990) referred to as an "outsider-within perspective," the women were always aware of life on the other side of their world. They addressed racism by name as a power that constrained them and, in describing their lives, they painted pictures of an endurance that has been configured by gender subordination. The limiting influence of class was not explicitly spoken of by all of the women, but it was however, directly apparent in all the women's lives, either because of present economic hardships or because of their present perspective that was influenced by the impoverished circumstances of their youth.

The obstacles that they encountered in school were no different than those experienced in the other three areas. To cope with old dilemmas, the women relied on familiar strategies they had used throughout their lives. The strategies of silence, negotiation, and resistance were used by the women to cope with and respond to the direct impact of racism, sexism, and classism. A very important finding in this study was that Black women employed the concept of ethgender (Ranson & Miller, 1983) in thinking of and describing themselves. This idea sets forth that gender and ethnicity are tightly fused in the conscious mind and that they can not be conceived of separately. The respondents consistently conceptualized the fact of gender and race simultaneously and overwhelmingly spoke of being a "Black woman" and rarely referred to being a woman or Black without accompanying descriptors.

Summary

Overall the women characterized their reentry episodes as chilling experiences and depicted academia as hostile. Their stories, which included their social, familial, and classroom encounters, were tales of marginality and isolation. The major themes revealed in the reentry narratives of the women studied were that race and gender oppression overwhelmingly affected them both inside and outside of the classroom. Another theme that emerged involved how the participants' lives were also constrained by class issues. However, this theme was seen as more peripheral to the reentry process.

The narratives of Black reentry women in this study added a new detail to the profile of the reentry student. Viewing Black women as a separate research group, apart from the category of women and Blacks, widens and sharpens the research lens by allowing the researcher to address issues of race and gender simultaneously. By examining the lives of Black reentry women through qualitative means, the data revealed a detailed appraisal of Black reentry women using their own thoughts and words to give them reality and voice. Placing Black women at the center of research on reentry women eliminates the need to extrapolate about them based on previously collected data that neglected to sample them. Black women represent an untapped source of significant research opportunity as a correlational lens through which many dynamics can be simultaneously studied. Viewing Black women as a separate entity or including issues of race, gender, class, and color, does not crowd or dilute the research agenda nor does it skew the focus from Blacks, women, or Whites. It merely enriches the research picture.

The following guide was used to conduct the interviews.

Interview Guide

Opening Statement

I am very interested in what happens to Black women in school, both as girls and as women. I would like to ask you questions about your school experiences. Although I will be asking questions and seeking answers from you, I want you to feel free to take your time in answering the questions and feel free to refuse to answer any question. My intention is to learn about your story. I am a Black woman who loves to listen and to talk and it is my hope that this interview will be fun.

Sample Questions

Questions About the Overall Experience

1. What is your most pleasant memory of school?
2. How would you describe your overall school experience?
3. What one word would you use to describe you entire school experience?
4. What is your most painful memory of school?

Questions About the Higher Education Experience

5. Why is it important to you to earn the higher education degree you are pursuing?
6. Who were your most important influences in school?
7. Who or what were your negative influences in school?
8. If you were asked to explain your higher education experiences by comparing them to something else, what phrase or group of words would you use?
9. What teacher influenced you the most?
10. Did you have a mentor during this time?
11. Tell me what a typical school day was like for you by walking me through it.
12. Who was your support or confidant during this process?
13. How do you see yourself as a student?
14. Do you think your teachers have been fair to you in their assessment of your work and abilities?
15. How has the educational endeavor affected your personal relationships?
16. What role has education played in the lives of your family of origin?
17. Is there anything else that you would like to talk about that I have neglected to ask?

References

Alexander, I. E. (1988). Personality, psychological assessment, and psychobiography. In D. P. McAdams, & R. L. Ochberg (Eds.), *Psychobiography and life narratives* (pp. 265–294). Durham: Duke University Press.

Amott, T. L., & Matthaei, J. A. (Eds.). (1991). *Race, gender & work: A multicultural economic history of women in the United States*. Boston: South End Press.

Anderson, R. E., & Darkenwald, G. G. (1979). *Participation and persistence in American adult education*. New York: College Board.

Beer, C. T. (1989). Returning women: Their perceptions of the social environment of the classroom. *Initiatives, 52*(1), 11–17.

Bogdan, R. C., & Biklen, S. K. (1982). *Qualitative research for education: An introduction to theory and methods*. Boston: Allyn and Bacon.

Caffarella, R. S., & Olson, S. K. (1993). Psychosocial development of women: A critical review of the literature. *Adult Education Quarterly, 43*(3), 125–151.

Carp, A., Peterson, R., & Roelfs, P. (1974). Adult learning interests and experiences. In K. P. Cross, J. R. Valley, & Associates (Eds.), *Planning non-traditional programs: An analysis of the issues for postsecondary education* (pp. 11–52). San Francisco: Jossey-Bass.

Casey, L. (1993). *I answer with my life: Life histories of women teachers working for social change*. New York: Routledge.

Collins, P. H. (1989). The social construction of Black feminist thought. *Signs, 14*(4), 745–773.

Collins, P. H. (1990). *Black feminist thought: Knowledge, consciousness, and the politics of empowerment*. New York: Routledge.

Cross, P. K. (1981). *Adults as learners: Increasing participation and facilitating learning*. San Francisco: Jossey-Bass.

Cuthbert, M. V. (1942/1987). *Education and marginality: A study of the Negro woman college graduate*. New York: Garland Press.

Davis, A. Y. (1981). *Women, race, and class*. New York: Bantam Books.

Demos, P. (1979). *A career counseling survey of reentry program for women*. Berkeley: California State University.

Denzin, N. (1989). *Interpretive biography*. Newbury Park, CA: Sage.

DuBois, W. E. B. (1903/1953). *The souls of Black folk*. Greenwich: Fawcett.

Etter-Lewis, G. (1993). *My soul is my own: Oral narratives of African American women in the professions*. New York: Routledge.

Evangelauf, J. (1992). Separate studies list top disciplines, big producers of minority graduates: Earned degrees. *Chronicle of Higher Education, 38*(36), A36–37.

Fleming, J. (1984). *Blacks in college: A comparative study of student success in Black and in White institutions*. San Francisco: Jossey-Bass.

Frazier, E. F. (1962). *The Black bourgeois*. New York: Collier.

Giddings, P. (1984). *When and where I enter: The impact of Black women on race and sex in America*. New York: Bantam Books.

Gilligan, C. (1982). *In a different voice: Psychological theory and women's development*. Cambridge, MA: Harvard University Press.

Gluck, S. B., & Patai, D. (Eds.). (1991). *Women's words: The feminist practice of oral history*. New York: Routledge.

Hacker, A. (1992). *Two nations: Black and White, separate, hostile, unequal*. New York: Ballantine Books.

Hall, R. M., & Sandler, B. R. (1982). The classroom climate: A chilly one for women? *Project on the Status and Education of Women*. Washington, D.C.: Association of American Colleges.

Harrington, T. S. (1993). Why they stay: A study on the persistence of reentry women. *Initiatives, 55*(4), 17–24.

Henry, M. D. (1985). Black reentry females: Their concerns and needs. *Journal of the National Association for Women Deans, Administrators, and Counselors, 48*(4), 5–10.

hooks, b. (1984). *From margin to center*. Boston: South End Press.

hooks, b. (1989). *Talking back: Thinking feminist, thinking Black*. Boston: South End Press.

Hull, G. T., Scott, P., & Smith, B. (Eds.). (1982). *All the women are White, All the men are Black: But some of us are brave*. New York: Feminist Press.

Johnson-Bailey, J. (1994). *Making a way out of no way: An analysis of the educational narratives of reentry Black women with emphasis on issues of race, gender, class, and color* (Unpublished doctoral dissertation, The University of Georgia, 1994).

Johnstone, J. W., & Rivera, R. J. (1965). *Volunteers for learning*. Chicago: Aldine.

Kaplan, S. R. (1982). A feminist Cinderella tale: Women over thirty in graduate and professional school. *Journal of the National Association for Women Deans, Administrators, and Counselors, 45*, 9–15.

Lewis, L. H. (Ed.). (1988). *Addressing the needs of returning women*. San Francisco: Jossey-Bass.

Lorde, A. (1984). *Sister outsider: Essays & speeches*. Freedom, CA: The Crossing Press.

Luttrell, W. (1993). "The teachers, they all had their pets:" Concepts of gender, knowledge, and power. *Signs, 18*(3), 505–546.

McAdams, D. P. (1988). Biography, narrative, and lives: An introduction. In D. P. McAdams & R. L. Ochberg (Eds.), *Psychobiography and life narratives* (pp. 1–18). Durham, NC: Duke University Press.

Merriam, S. B., & Caffarella, R. S. (1991). *Learning in adulthood*. San Francisco: Jossey-Bass.

Noble, J. L. (1956). *The Negro woman's college education*. New York: Bureau of Publications Teacher's College.

Ochberg, R. L. (1988). Life stories and the psychosocial construction of careers. In D. P. McAdams & R. L. Ochberg (Eds.), *Psychobiography and life narratives* (pp. 173–204). Durham, NC: Duke University Press.

Pierre, S. S. (1989). Understanding the nontraditional female student. *National Association of Student Personal Administration, 26*(3), 228–234.

Pitts, S. P. (1992). Reentry women in higher education: The quiet revolution. *College Student Affairs Journal, 12*(1), 69–75.

Player, W. B. (1948/1987). *Improving college education for women at Bennett College.* New York: Garland Press.

Ransford. E. H., & Miller, J. (1983). Race, sex, and feminist outlooks. *American Journal of Sociology, 48,* 46–59.

Riessman, C. K. (1993). *Narrative analysis.* Newbury Park, CA: Sage.

Rifenbary, D. (1995). Reentering the academy: The voices of returning women students. *Initiatives, 55*(4), 17–24.

Russell, K., Wilson, M., & Hall, R. (1992). *The color complex.* New York: Doubleday.

Sadker, M., & Sadker, D. (1994). *Failing at fairness: How America's schools cheat girls.* New York: Charles Scribner's Sons.

Safman, P. C. (1988). Women from special populations: The challenge of reentry. In L. Lewis (Ed.), *Addressing the needs of returning women* (pp. 79–94). San Francisco: Jossey-Bass.

Schmittroth, L. (Ed.). 1995. *Statistical record of women worldwide* (2nd ed.) New York: Gale Research Inc.

Scott, K. Y. (1991). *The habit of surviving.* New York: Ballantine.

Teachman, J., & Paasch, K. (1989). Returning to school after marriage: Results for Whites and Blacks. *Sociological Forum, 4*(3), 423–433.

Tittle, C. K., & Denker, E. R. (1980). *Returning women students in higher education.* New York: Praeger.

Touchton, J., & Davis, L. (1991). *Fact book on women in higher education.* New York: Macmillan.

Wallace, M. (1978). *Black macho and the myth of the superwoman.* New York: Dial Press.

Weinberg, M. (1977). *A chance to learn: The history of race and education in the United States.* Cambridge: Cambridge University Press.

Witherell, C., & Noddings, N. (1991). *Stories lives tell: Narrative dialogue in education.* New York: Teachers College Press.

ANNOTATED BIBLIOGRAPHY

The following books are offered with accompanying summaries and critiques in order to provide the reader with information about Black women's experiences. It is believed that these texts are applicable to the lives of the reentry women in this study. They have been particularly useful in higher education research and survey courses and have been of special significance to me personally and professionally.

Bell-Scott, P. (1995). *Life Notes: Personal writings of contemporary Black women.* New York: Norton.

A collection of journal writings that detail how race and gender, being a Black woman in America, affect the life stories of everyday African American women. The personal accounts cover critical events in these women's life spans: childhood, adolescence, and adulthood. Examples of how women, who have been faced with physical and psychological violence, discrimination, and overwhelming structural inequalities, have managed, fought, survived, and triumphed are included in this text.

Boyd, J. A. (1993). *In the company of my sisters: Black women and self esteem.* New York: Dutton.

Through stories from her childhood and tales from other women, Julia Boyd examines the barriers Black women must face in society and how these difficulties impact self-esteem. Issues discussed include the portrayal of Black women in the media, body-image, messages received from our family of origin, and intimacy issues.

Cleage, P. (1993). *Deals with the devil and other reasons to riot.* New York: Ballantine.

Cleage speaks directly about life in America as a Black woman. She discusses violence against women and gives advice on coping. She writes candidly about everything from colorism to Black conservatives to Black manhood.

Collins, P. H. (1990). *Black feminist thought: Knowledge, consciousness, and the politics of empowerment.* New York: Routledge.

This text is considered a definitive work on Black women's ways of knowing. Collins examines the historical underpinnings of Black women's theoretical and epistemological standpoints and discusses how they have influenced Black women's existence.

Etter-Lewis, G. (1993). *My soul is my own: Oral narratives of African-American women in the professions.* New York: Routledge.

Nine Black women's narratives give voice to the struggles of Black women working in the professions. Musicians, professors, social workers, historians and physicians discuss their lives and their work. The narratives are followed by Etter-Lewis's essays on women in higher education and the professions.

Feagin, J. R., & Sikes, M. P. (1994). *Living with racism: The black middle-class experience.* Boston: Beacon Press.
The authors detail the racist experiences of middle-class Blacks in today's America. Of particular interest is the chapter titled "Seeking a Good Education." Over 200 Black participants were interviewed for this book.

Giddings, P. (1984). *When and where I enter: The impact of Black women on race and sex in America.* New York: Bantam Books.
The narrative history of Black women in America unfolds through interviews, letters, papers and other historical documents. Transcending the double discrimination of race and gender in America is a prominent theme in the book.

Guy-Sheftall, B. (Ed.). (1995). *Words of fire: An anthology of African-American feminist thought.* New York: New Press.
This collection of essays contains the struggles and wisdom of Black feminists from the 1830s to present. Early writings defining race and sex are followed by essays addressing the definition of Black womanhood. Racial/sexual politics, Black women and feminism, and writings on resistance are also included.

Hine, D. C., King, W., & Reed, L. (1995). *We specialize in the wholly impossible: A reader in Black women's history.* New York: Carson.
A history reader that contains thirty-two essays about historical events or movements in which African American women were either leaders or significant contributors. The work spans U.S. history and places Black women firmly in context in the Revolutionary War, the original Women's Movement, and other major U.S. events.

hooks, b. (1989). *Talking back: Thinking feminist, thinking black.* Boston: South End Press.
bell hooks writes about feminist consciousness, her experiences as a Black woman in graduate school, the intersection of class and education, overcoming white supremacy, and homophobia in the Black community among other subjects. Her engaging style and frank presentation make good reading.

hooks, b. (1993). *Sisters of the yam: Black women and self-recovery.* Boston: South End Press.
The well-being of Black women is discussed. hooks addresses the "how-tos" of self-recovery and writes on forgiveness, spirituality and work. Chapters include "Living to Love," "Work Makes Life Sweet" and "Knowing Peace: An End to Stress."

hooks, b. (1996). *Bone black: Memories of girlhood.* New York: Henry Holt.

This book is the story of bell hooks's memories of her girlhood in the South. The intersection of race, class and gender is seen in these remembrances of years past. The short chapters are packed with thought-provoking reflections.

Hull, G., Scott, P. B., & Smith, B. (1982). *All the women are White, all the Blacks are men, but some of us are brave: Black women's studies.* New York: Feminist Press.

This book heralded the presence of Black women as a neglected but present force in Women's Studies programs in the academy. The editors of this book discuss in twenty-eight chapters the components of Black feminism and give an in-depth analysis of how African American women fare in higher education as faculty and students.

Johnson-Bailey, J. (1999). Black Reentry Women in the Academy: Making a Way Out of No Way. *Initiatives, 58*(4), 37–48.

This article examines academic narratives of eight reentry Black women. It looks specifically at the coping mechanisms they used in their schooling: silence, resistance, and negotiation.

Johnson-Bailey, J. (1999). Participation and Retention Concerns of Black Women Adult Learners. In D. Ntiri (Ed.), *Pedagogy for Adult Learners: Methods and Strategies* (pp.7–34). Detroit: Wayne State University Press.

This article isolates the participation and retention concerns of ten Black undergraduate and graduate women. It examines the power dynamics that occur in the classroom around the issues of race, gender, and class.

Lawrence-Lightfoot, S. (1988). *Balm in Gilead: Journey of a healer.* New York: Penguin Books.

A biography of one of the first Black women to graduate from Cornell University and Columbia's University School of Medicine to become a physician. This book is about a Black woman, born at the turn of the century, who struggled to earn an education and make her way as a child psychiatrist in New York City. Written by her daughter, a noted author and scholar, the work contains special insights that are presented through the lenses of daughter, mother, scholar, and activist.

Lawrence-Lightfoot, S. (1994). *I've known rivers: Lives of loss and liberation.* Reading, MA: Addison-Wesley.

A compilation of six life stories of extraordinary African Americans. Lawrence-Lightfoot introduces the reader to the adult and contemporary dilemmas faced by men and women who made courageous strides in an effort to achieve their dreams or to work towards a goal. The stories include: a woman Presbyterian minister; a woman radio tycoon, and a Black male lawyer on the Anita Hill legal team.

Madison, D. S. (Ed.). (1994). *The woman that I am: The literature and culture of contemporary women of color.* New York: St. Martin's Press.

Madison has compiled a collection of poetry, short stories, drama and cultural narratives. Themes discussed include: the transition from girlhood to womanhood, issues of race, class and justice, and being a woman. Authors include Toni Cade Bambara, Amy Tan, Audre Lorde, and Bharati Mukherjee.

Nelson, J. (1993). *Volunteer slavery: My authentic Negro experience.* New York: Penguin Books.

Jill Nelson's experiences of discrimination as the first Black woman writer at the *Washington Post* are interspersed with earlier happenings as a Black woman in America. Nelson candidly writes about the many forms of discrimination she experienced at the paper. Her humor is evident throughout.

Scott, K. S. (1991). *The habit of surviving.* New York: Ballantine.

Scott invites Marilyn, Sara, Elaine and Gwen to tell their stories of survival as Black women growing up in the 1940s and 1950s. These powerful life histories are augmented by Scott's presentation of Black women's cultural history and Scott's presentation of habits of surviving.

Walker, A. (1997). *Anything we love can be saved: A writer's activism.* New York: Random House. Walker presents a book that details the difficulties she has encountered in pursuing her work as an author writing about controversial subjects, such as race, gender, and sexual orientation. This work has life relevance as Walker makes concrete parallels between the struggles she faces and the issues that are faced by many women, particularly Black women.

Wilson, M., & Russell, K. (1998). *Divided sisters: Bridging the gap between Black women and White women.* New York: Anchor Books.

An accessible yet scholarly text that presents research and real life stories on the complex nature of the relationship between Black and White women. The authors, a Black woman and White woman, give personal looks into how the history of these two groups of women haunt their contemporary relationships.

Related Academic References

Broach, T. J. (1984). Concerns of Black women and White women returning to school (Doctoral dissertation, University of Florida, 1984). *Dissertation Abstracts International, 46-03A*:0611.

Bunce, S. H. (1996). "It's always something": African-American women's college reentry experience (Unpublished doctoral dissertation, University of Southern California, 1996). *Dissertation Abstracts International, 58-01A*:0302.

Carter, D., Pearson, C., & Shavlik, D. (1987–1988). Double jeopardy: Women of color in higher education. *Educational Record, 68*(4) & *69*(1), 98–103.

Cuthbert, M. V. (1942/1987). *Education and marginality: A study of the Negro woman college graduate.* NY: Garland Press.

Everhart, R. B. (1983). *Reading, writing and resistance.* Boston: Routledge & Kegan Paul.

Fleming, J. (1984). *Blacks in college: A comparative study of student success in Black and in White institutions.* San Francisco: Jossey-Bass.

Grant, L. (1992). Race and the schooling of young girls. In J. Wrigley (Ed.), *Education and gender equality* (pp. 91–113). Washington, DC: Falmer Press.

Hall, R. M., & Sandler, B. R. (1982). *The classroom climate: A chilly one for women?* Project on the Status and Education of Women, Washington, DC: Association of American Colleges.(ERIC Document Reproduction Service No. ED 215 628).

Henry, M. D. (1985). Black reentry females: Their concerns and needs. *Journal of the National Association for Women Deans, Administrators, and Counselors, 48*(4), 5–10.

Ihle, E. L. (1986). *Black women's academic education in the South: History of black women's education in the South, 1865–Present.* (Report No: UD-025-516). Harrisonburg, VA: James Madison University. (ERIC Document Reproduction Service No. ED 281 959).

Johnson-Bailey, J. (1994). *Making a way out of no way: An analysis of the educational narratives of reentry Black women with emphasis on issues of race, gender, class and color.* Unpublished doctoral dissertation, The University of Georgia, Athens.

Johnson-Bailey, J. (1998). Black reentry women in the academy: Making a way out of no way. *Initiatives, 58*(4), 37–48.

Lewter, A. J. (1995). Diamonds in the rough: A case study of college transfer African American reentry females at Halifax Community College. (Doctoral dissertation, North Carolina State University, 1995). *Dissertation Abstracts International, 56-04A*:1212.

Luttrell, W. (1989). Working-class women's ways of knowing: Effects of gender, race, and class. *Sociology of Education, 62*(1), 33–46.

Luttrell, W. (1993). "The teachers, they all had their pets": Concepts of gender, knowledge, and power. *Signs, 18*(3), 505–546.

Margolis, E., & Romero, M. (1998). "The department is very male, very White, very old, and very conservative": The functioning of the hidden curriculum in graduate Sociology departments. *Harvard Educational Review, 68*(1), 1–32.

Miller, E. L. (1997). Fears expressed by female reentry students at an urban community college: A qualitative study. (Doctoral dissertation, Teachers College, Columbia University, 1997). *Dissertation Abstracts International, 58-09A*:3393.

Moses, Y. T. (1989). *Black women in academe: Issues and strategies* (Report No.: HE-022-909). Washington, DC: Project on the Status and Education of Women, Association of American Colleges. (ERIC Document Reproduction Service No. ED 311 817).

Noble, J. L. (1956). *The Negro woman's college education.* NY: Bureau of Publications, Teacher's College.

Player, W. B. (1987). *Improving college education for women at Bennett College: A report of a type A project.* NY: Garland Press.

Reskin, B., & Roos, P. (1990). *Job queues, gender queues.* Philadelphia: Temple University Press.

Solomon, B. M. (1985). *In the company of educated women: A history of women and higher education in America.* New Haven, CT: Yale University Press.

Ward, W. G. (1997). Black female graduate students in the Academy: Re-moving the masks (Report No. HE-030-314). Washington, DC. (ERIC Document Reproduction Service No. ED 410 779).

Washington, V. (1988). *The power of Black women: Progress, predicaments and possibilities* (Report No.: HE-022-826). Albany, NY: Association of Black Women in Higher Education, Inc. (ERIC Document Reproduction Service No. ED 323 821).

Withorn, A. (1986). Dual citizenship: An interview with women of color in graduate school. *Women's Studies Quarterly, 25*(1&2), 132–138.